INSIGHTS INTO THE *KI* PERSONALITIES IN POLITICS AND THE MEDIA

THE 9 KI PERSONALITY TYPES

Sally Fretwell

Feng Shui Unlimited

Sally Fretwell/Feng Shui Unlimited
www.Kipersonalities.com

INSIGHTS INTO THE KI PERSONALITIES IN POLITICS AND THE MEDIA
Sally Fretwell 1st ed.
ISBN 978-0-9721548-8-8

Dedicated to all the people who strive to understand who they are and what they are here to do.

"Associate yourself with men of good quality, if you esteem your own reputation; for 'tis better to be alone than in bad company."

—

George Washington

TABLE OF CONTENTS

The *2 EARTH* Personality—*The Expressive.*
Depicted by all forms of emotion: joy, sadness, anger, fear, and shame. This type is about "The Story."

> ***Masters at crafting the story:***
> **Media Moguls, Oprah Winfrey, and Saul Alinsky.** The *9 Fire, 2 Earth* personality type. **Alan Greenspan**, a *2 Earth, 1 Water* personality type.

The *3 TREE* Personality—*The Thunderous*
Depicted by the explosive nature of a storm: loud, often referred to as a *clap*, *crack*, *peal of thunder*, or *boom.*

> **Sean Hannity** and **Ann Coulter**, *3 Tree, 4 Tree* types, **Newt Gingrich**, a *1 Water, 3 Tree* type, and **Sebastian Gorka**, a *3 Tree, 6 Metal* type.

The *4 TREE* Personality—*The Wind*
Depicted by a soft breeze, a burst, a gust, a whirlwind, or a gale: a force of moving air, able to reach faraway lands.

The *5 EARTH* Personality—*The Center*

Depicted by the Earth, the surface that serves as the center for plants, water, and all of life. A Gatherer.

> **Rush Limbaugh**, a *5 Earth, 9 Fire* type, **Mark Steyn**, a *5 Earth, 1 Water* type, **Mike Pence**, a *5 Earth, 7 Metal* type, and **James Mattis**, a *5 Earth, 4 Tree* type.

The *6 METAL* Personality—*The Conduit*

Depicted by the current of movement: a channel or vessel for moving energy, like a bolt or a train on tracks.

> **Kellyanne Conway**, a *7 Metal, 6 Metal* type.

The *7 METAL* Personality—*The Pragmatist*

Depicted by motion below the surface: the nuts and bolts or an energy connecting all pieces together.

> **Mark Levin**, a *7 Metal, 1 Water* type, and **Jay Sekulow**, an *8 Earth, 7 Metal* type.

The *8 EARTH* Personality—*The Introspect*

Depicted by the stillness deep inside a mountain: quiet movement that is gentle on the outside and strong and solid on the inside.

> **Hillary Clinton**, an *8 Earth, 3 Tree* type, and **John Kelly**, a *5 Earth, 8 Earth* type.

The *9 FIRE* Personality—*The Flamboyant*
Depicted by the flames of fire: a flickering, mesmerizing, blazing, burning, bright, hot inferno.

Why **Bill Clinton**, a *9 Fire, 8 Earth* type, **George Bush**, a *1 Water, 9 Fire* type, and **Barack Obama**, a *3 Tree 9 Fire* type, were easily able to become president.

Mike Huckabee and Sarah H. Sanders, *9 Fire, 8 Earth* types.

PREFACE

Every person is unique. No two people are exactly alike. When we consider a person's nationality, religion, homeland, and life style, we see how they all create a filter for life experience.

Our upbringing certainly influences how we express ourselves in the world and affects how we navigate through everyday life. In today's world, the media uses "bombarding social media" to influence us emotionally and ultimately to try to shape how we filter what happens around us. Despite these various influences, there are still common strands of human experience. My goal is to show that even though we all have different experiences in life, there are very distinct personality types.

Based on the *I Ching,* an ancient Taoist text, we each have unique personality traits that assist us on our paths in life. Our potentials, our strengths and weaknesses are easy to see when we grasp the insights of this ancient text. The *I Ching* was used to predict that Donald Trump would be president because of the circumstances of this time. However, the *I Ching* is less a book of predictions than a study of nature.

Human nature follows nature, so we can say that these fascinating and predictable personality types serve as a base to understand what energizes and drains a person. I will use my insights from the ancient Taoist teachings, to show how to recognize personality types in the media and politics.

We all have a **Ki personality**; it is a surface expression of who we are. It is how we interact with others in our day-to-day life. It is the first impressions we give when others meet us for the first time. When people get to know us a little better, they may get a glimpse into the side of us that is not easily seen right away.

Say you try a new coffee shop. The way you move through the coffee shop and how quickly you ask for your order are part of the way you express yourself. This is the **energy**, the **Ki**, *that* you were born with.

As people get to know you better, they start to see your **Inner Ki** nature, which includes your thoughts, feelings, and motivations. Our **Inner Ki** nature is

often unseen and guides our inner lives. This nature
is stronger in our younger years and when we are
stressed or under pressure. Children that have a
stressful or rough childhood tend to grow up faster
and navigate the world less in touch with their
inner *Ki* personality. Incorporating these two
natures is needed to create balance.

Our personality is made up of multiple facets that
each makes us who we are. Ancient Taoist
philosophers and astronomers observed nature and
the predictable cycles that occur in our Universe.
They watched how people and all living things cycle
in the same way. These cycles can be seen in
connection with the moon cycle, the sun cycle, the
earth's rotation, the seasons, day and night, and
many other natural cycles. A woman's cycle is close
to a 28-day cycle, which is related to the predictable
moon cycle, or what the medical world would call
"regular."

They observed the cycles of the best time to plant
crops, and how that coincided with harvesting those
crops. They noted which side of a mountain was

best for building to take advantage of the sun. They noticed that spring was related to the springing up of the new plants. They recorded the way the sun moved across the sky, and how this timing was crucial to the success of all life. Today, we take these cycles for granted and have lost the need to study and harness the many energy cycles that still exist.

In a very basic way, all life is affected by these cycles. When in balance with these cycles, salmon know when to swim up the river to spawn, bears know when to hibernate, and birds know when to fly south. Seeds push out of the ground, expand, and search for the sun, beginning their growth. If nurtured, a plant continues through this predictable cycle that all life has the potential to follow. We all know this life-to-death cycle well. The seasons also follow it: winter is a dormant time of year, when the sun is in a position of less light; this is opposed to summer, a time of more light and more growth.

Our birthdays form a yearly cycle whose arrival we recognize. Each day cycles, and during the day our energy cycles. Some of us are charged up in the

morning and start to fade in the afternoon. Others
are up late into the night and have no energy in the
morning. The more you understand your own daily
cycle, the more you can take advantage of the
energy that supports your well-being.

CHAPTER 1

The Origin of the personality types. THE *KI,* our energy.

The ancient Taoists saw a distinct correlation between the time of year and the cycle of energy. Because of this correlation, the time a person is born is related to the energy cycle. They saw this distinct pattern and studied the specific season and year in which a person was born. Doing this created insights and more in-depth observation of a person's *Inner KI nature.*

Since it was observed that we have two vital **KI** energy cycles in our personality, the interaction of each with the other is of great importance. The more you understand and can utilize your innate birth **Ki**, the better you will be.

This is especially helpful when interacting with others. This does not mean that all people with the same personality type are exactly the same, but it does mean that they share the same tools in their toolbox.

You can see very distinct qualities, strengths, and weaknesses in each of the personality type combinations. This explains why you are more in sync with some people but not at all with others. However, that it as topic for another book.

I will use historical figures and people in the media and politics as comparisons to make my point. I have used this system for over 25 years and it has served me well in helping my clients understand themselves, as well as their friends, family, and co-workers.

There are 9 personality types, but I hesitate to put too much importance on that number until one understands the relationship between a person's inner and outer natures, which is where real revelations can be made.

There are 81 personality type combinations. Some people are perfectly in sync with themselves. In this case, one part of their personality supports the other.

In contrast, others are polarized or swing from one side of their personality to the other. Second-guessing themselves, they are always searching for clarity. Often, these are the people who beat themselves up for the choices they make.

With this system, you can see what a person can do to balance their lives and build a path forward for peace and clarity by seeing their strength and weaknesses.

Chi, or *Ki*, means LIFE FORCE

This system is based on the same principles as
Acupuncture, Chinese medicine, macrobiotics, and
Ayurvedic medicine. Martial arts, Qigong, and Tai
Chi are all related to the study of energy and how it
moves through the body. Many of the older sciences
and medical modalities can be traced to the same
principles. It also addresses how everything moves
in cycles and when everything flows in balance. Like
the stock market, which goes up and then down, all
things are ever changing.

Anyone who practices martial arts knows they are
all about calculation, moving consciously and
efficiently. The teacher shows the student where he
needs to be to maximize his energy. Balance is
always the goal, so using the power of energy
requires continual study.

Wu of Hsia, an ancient engineer, brought
prosperity to the townsmen by using the
understanding of elements in nature to situate the
village and to reconfigure the river to support the

people. He observed the weather, how the sun moved across the sky, where the best place was to plant the crops, and how they could harness energy to support their existence. Survival was the motivating factor. All the elements cycle, and when in balance they support, nurture, and circulate energy.

Understanding the elements means understanding what builds energy and what drains energy. This is true in the personality types as well, and what creates balance in each personality type. This system is similarly used in diagnosing and treating ailments in Chinese medicine and macrobiotics. Balancing energy flow in the meridians brings forth optimal health.

Harnessing Your Potential

I have always been fascinated by what makes people tick. I grew up in a family that most would describe as unusual, and my dad was quite a character. He was an athletic individual who felt everyone needed to be physically fit and work hard. He knew his body was a vessel on which he desperately relied to get through life in the 1920s.

Being very disciplined, he was the captain of the football team. Most of his fraternity brothers also played on the Nebraska football team and they knew that "Dirty George" was dedicated to keeping the team in tiptop shape. He went on to play for the

Green Bay Packers and flew 52 bomber missions in WW2 in the Pacific.

He was the top wrestler at the school and even when he was in his mid-70s, he would challenge Navy Seals at the ice cream shop to a push up contest. He once challenged 3 Seals entering his favorite ice cream shop that if they could do more push-ups then he could, he would buy them each an ice cream of their choice. All three chuckled and did as many as they could and then watched with a smile as he did even more. They all bought him an ice cream.

My dad is the personality type *3 Tree, 4 Tree*. Once I understood the *I Ching*, that made perfect sense to me. I could totally see the gifts, challenges, and especially insights in our family dynamic. It totally made sense to me why his personality type, *3 Tree, 4 Tree*, navigates the world the way it does. Depicted by the *I Ching*, trigrams expressed his nature as loud like *Thunder* and a whirlwind like the *Wind.*

My interest broadened to include the psychology of architecture, and why people feel good in some places and not in others. Why can some buildings, for example, a hospital, feel oppressive and even do the opposite of helping a person to heal and restore well-being?

I was fascinated by why some people do best when they are by the water, while others thrive when they are in the mountains; why some people have a hard time calming down or why some cannot get motivated. This is the same as how some jobs are perfect for one person but not for another.

I have spent nearly 30 years helping people create spaces that support their well-being. Part of that is giving them the insights I have gleaned from an ancient system that I spent years studying and observing.

This system does not explain what has happened to us in our lives, but it does explain what makes us tick. It looks at how we come across to others, and gives clarity and observations into our unseen inner emotional natures.

The system explains why some people are "outgoing" on the surface, but may be the opposite on the inside. After sharing insights with my clients for over 25 years, I still get feedback that the insights I offered have made all the difference in their lives. I often say to my clients that they cannot pick their family, but why not have greater clarity and appreciation for themselves and those around them.

Even my daughter, who disagrees with me on many things like politics, will have her friends call me when they are starting a new relationship to see if they will be compatible. Of course, I do not say that some people are good and some people are not, but some people are more compatible and others are not, even with themselves. This goes for hiring new employees as well.

This system gives validity to why we each navigate life in our own ways and why some people seem to be in alignment with themselves and others seem

discombobulated, constantly re-evaluating
decisions they make.

Sure, horrible things can happen to a person in life
that can affect that person negatively. My point is
that what I have learned explains why Dirty
George's **3 Tree, 4 Tree** thunderous personality
could fly a plane in WW2, have 9 men shot and die
in his plane, and still see things in life the way he
did. He is a hard-core quirky individual, but he is
great to have in your corner. Each combination of
personality types has associated strengths and
weaknesses associated, meaning certain things
build their energy and certain things drain their
energy.

It is essential to have less judgment and more
freedom to be who you are. You may never be the
best at something that you think you should be good
at. Some people are great at starting things and
getting the ball rolling, but horrible at finishing
things. Some are great at keeping things in line, but
have a hard time letting go and having fun. Some
people are perceived a certain way, like stuffy, when

they are not that at all. This can happen regardless of motivation, IQ, or strength of intention.

We all have had relationships with family members that are painstakingly hard, while others are so easy. These easier relationships are greater and less personal; less time is put into trying to change those around you. Whether you are the youngest or the oldest in the family, it is irrelevant to how you interface with yourself and others. Rather, it is about harnessing your **Ki** power.

I will use the *I CHING*'s wisdom to dissect well-known people in politics and the media using their personality types. Each of the personalities has strengths and weaknesses, but there is so much more to this system. I have witnessed clients that have had years of counselling say that, if they had understood their **KI** personality type, they would have been empowered to embrace what they have to offer the world.

It may be best to skim through this book and look at each of the **9 Personality types** to get a feel for what each personality is all about. Again, it is always a combination of two personality types that makes up a person's **KI** personality. Some people go through their whole lives expressing only one side of their nature. I have learned how to give a person insight into their full potential: their **KI** personality type.

CHAPTER 3

People Who Shaped the Election in Media and Politics

I will start by sharing information about the 45th president of the United States, **Donald J. Trump**, a **9 Fire, 1 Water** personality, and why he is loved by some and not by others. This is not just about politics, believe it or not. Without going into all 81 combinations of the personality types, I will talk about Donald Trump in a way that describes his nature using these personality types.

This will give you insights into why he is who he is and even why he is depicted as being two totally different people in one person. This is not because he is crazy, but because the two sides to his nature are very different. If you read about the **1 Water** personality type, which I describe in the next few pages, and read about the *9 Fire* personality later in the book, you will gain more clarity into the two very different expressions of his personality type. The *9 Fire* nature is very comfortable in the limelight, being on television, telling stories, insulting the media, and fanning the fires, so to speak. *9 Fire* personalities gain energy when on stage.

Donald Trump's inner *1 Water* nature is very low key: visionary, expansive, likes to be in the flow, contemplative, and a good listener. These qualities all exist in this one man. He is not acting; he actually has two very different sides to his nature. He can be very bold, forceful, and fiery, as well as very open, attentive, and free flowing. The *1 Water* nature can be a force to be reckoned with when riding a wave that they are passionate about.

Speaking from his inner compass, for instance on Sean Hannity's show, he talks about his love for the Country and things that matter to him. You would never think this is the same guy who is willing to call the media out when he feels they are not telling the truth. He speaks his truth, although his truth is not always calm and collected.

I knew the minute he announced he was running for president it would be quite a show based on his *I Ching* personality type. His visionary **1 Water** nature was seeing the bigger picture long before he decided to put himself in this position.

The part of his nature that is **9 Fire**, the part that loves the limelight, is often all you see. **Sean Hannity** and **Ann Coulter** both took the time to see deeper into Donald Trump's **1 Water** visionary side: the person who they had begun to appreciate and who really did want to make America great again. Whether you agree with him or not does not matter.

Both **Sean Hannity** and **Ann Coulter**, **3 Tree**, **4 Tree** personalities who I will discuss when I discuss the **3 Tree** personality, saw the dynamic combination that Donald Trump offered people in today's world. They gleaned a view into the two very different sides to Trump's personality. His fiery, **9 *Fire***, larger-than-life side of his personality, loving the limelight, combined with his visionary, expansive, ***1 Water*** nature.

Donald Trump would need people around him like Ann and Sean, ***3 Tree, 4 Tree*** types, because they stay on message; they are like Jack Russell terriers pulling at pant legs, keeping their eyes focused on the ball. People that see the value, follow the facts, and investigate the issues benefit a personality like Donald Trump because that is not where his strengths are.

Ann Coulter and **Sean Hannity**, **3 *Tree*, 4 *Tree*** personality types, bring out the best in Donald Trump. At the same time, they have the ability to share things in a verbally sensible and clear way. Each of us has relationships that are very comfortable and easy, as well as relationships that are uncomfortable and abrasive.

Being on the campaign trail was a breeze for Donald Trump; the excitement fueled him and inspired him to fight for the people. His **9 *Fire*** nature loved to tell stories and add dramatic presentation. This provided a great way for him to share his *1 Water* vision and belief that the country was going in the wrong direction. He is a polarizing figure, and if you do not look a bit deeper all you can see is his *9 Fire* nature, which can be interpreted as simply that of a showman. His *1 Water* nature is what drew in the crowds, who followed his drive and vision. I discuss the *1 Water* personality in the next chapter and the *9 Fire* personality later in the book.

Melania Trump, *3 Tree, 3 Tree*, is direct and can understand and support Trump's goals. She speaks her mind and would be a good partner for him from the *KI* personality perspective. The personality types manifest differently when you combine the inner nature with the outer nature.

The last 4 presidents have had *9 Fire* as either their outer nature or their inner emotional nature. Indeed, 19 out of 45 presidents have had the *Fire* nature in their personality type.

The 9 Personality types

The 1 WATER Personality

The Wave

In the *I Ching*, the water Trigram is depicted as the water personality. These qualities are represented in the vast expressions of water seen in nature: from the roar of the Sea, to the peace and flow of a bubbling stream, to the rage of a fast-moving river, and to the stagnation of a bog or swamp. Water also has the three states of liquid, solid, and gas. Mist, fog, rain clouds, and snow all relate to water in the form of precipitation.

Movement is always happening under the surface of any body of water. Unlimited potential exists to grow and support life in a water ecosystem. The Ocean is an ever-changing home to all sea life. It is a force to be reckoned with. The sea can be a dangerous body of water to cross, as well as peacefully calming.

This is also true in the *1 Water* personality. Underneath the surface, there is tremendous activity. This is an enduring personality, with great resilience and inner strength. There is a vast potential to learn, to be creative and expressive, and to follow a vision. The water personality houses the ability to be very prolific and expansive.

It is important for water personalities to be in the flow, and to feel fulfilled and uplifted by what they are doing. Otherwise, they get bogged down and stagnant. Fear, resentment, and being discontent are toxic, like "circling the drain," for a water person. When water is frozen, it limits what can exist in that environment; the flow stops and the water personality can become cold and frigid like ice. So, if you think of water in its many manifestations, you also can see the extreme expressions in this personality.

One minute they can be in the flow, expressive and easy going like a bubbling river. The next minute they can be fierce like the ocean. *1 Water* individuals are like the weather: it rains when the atmosphere is saturated with water. When they get overwhelmed, it is like a dam breaking: the water flows, filling and expanding over the banks that once held it back. There are so many variations of that overflow. Drizzle, hail, fog, condensation, dew, and mist are all ever changing and transforming into different states of expression.

Writers and journalists that have the *1 Water* personality are natural at writing and giving life both to ideas and the many characters that are often created in the minds of *1 Water* personalities. Writers and journalists that are *1 Water* personalities are often drawn to being on TV or radio, hosting shows, or writing for magazines. They use their ability to write and talk to express their thoughts. Dancing, singing, and free-flowing movement can all become expressions that a water personality would be at ease with.

Many of our media, TV, and Radio personalities are water personalities. They feel at home being a TV or radio host. This is playing out in the media today like never before. It is clear which TV and Radio personalities are on the left side of politics and which are on the right. Many of the *1 Water* personalities on the left were very relaxed in their reporting during the Obama administration.

When President Trump came into office, the same *1 Water* commentators shifted from being easy going, like Juan Williams, **a *1 Water, 6 Metal*** just bubbling along, to being the opposite, like a large Wave. Suddenly, they have no hesitation to express their feelings. See the *1 Water* personalities listed below. You can see this dynamic play out in politicians that are *1 Water* personalities as well.

Some of the most amazingly imaginative writers of our time have been water personalities. J.R.R. Tolkien, author of The Hobbit, and Madeleine L'Engle are *1 Water, 8 Earth* personalities that expressed their timeless imagination.

Jim Henson, creator of the Muppets, is a *1 Water, 1 Water*. These creators opened whole new worlds for us in their creations. George Westinghouse is a *1 Water, 1 Water*, personality, was an American entrepreneur and engineer who invented the railway air brake and was a pioneer of the electrical industry, gaining his first patent at the age of 19.

We all are familiar with Westinghouse products that are still in production today.

Charles Darwin, *1 Water, 8 Earth*, is another personality who was a visionary and delved into a deeper introspective perspective of why we are here.

Without going through the details of each personality, I will list each personality's inner and outer natures below. Keep in mind that it makes a big difference in how an individual will appear to the world if the water is in the outer personality or in the inner emotional nature.

1 WATER PERSONALITIES

	Outer Nature	Inner Nature
Mark Levin	7 Metal	1 Water
Dan Horowitz	7 Metal	1 Water
Eric Bolling	1 Water	6 Metal
Laura Ingraham	1 Water	4 Tree
Greta Van Susteren	1 Water	4 Tree
Dana Perino	1 Water	5 Earth

Mike Wallace	1 Water	5 Earth
Bernie Goldberg	1 Water	5 Earth
Shepard Smith	1 Water	6 Metal
Diane Sawyer	1 Water	7 Metal
Gail King	1 Water	7 Metal
Chris Matthews	1 Water	7 Metal
Buck Sexton	1 Water	7 Metal
Joe Scarborough	1 Water	6 Metal
Chuck Todd	1 Water	6 Metal
Juan Williams	1 Water	6 Metal
Andy Rooney	1 Water	6 Metal
Al Roker	1 Water	2 Earth
John McCain	1 Water	2 Earth
Joe diGenova	1 Water	8 Earth
Geraldo Rivera	3 Tree	1 Water
Mark Steyn	5 Earth	1 Water
C Krauthammer	5 Earth	1 Water
Charlie Rose	5 Earth	1 Water
Donna Brazile	5 Earth	1 Water
Bryant Gumbel	7 Metal	1 Water
Meredith Vieira	2 Earth	1 Water
Savannah Guthrie	2 Earth	1 Water

How these people express themselves is affected by the other personality type they have. For example, both **Savannah Guthrie** and **Meredith Vieira** share with emotion the story they are talking about. That comes from their *2 Earth, 1 Water* personalities, expressing their feelings and a detailed timeline.

Chris Matthews, *1 Water, 7 Metal*, and **Joe Scarborough** and **Chuck Todd,** *1 Water, 6 Metal*, all share a metal nature combined with a *1 Water* nature. Their intense metal nature is less obvious, but in this political environment, they have no problem whipping out their swords to do battle.

The same goes for **Mark Levin**; *7 Metal* is his outer nature, so he appears more outwardly intense, stating the facts and ready for battle. His *1 Water* expansive nature is less obvious in his presentation, but guides his ability to write and express his thoughts. A *1 Water* personality that is also a *6 or 7 Metal* is usually quick to act and easily moves forward on things he or she is passionate about.

Water personalities have the gift of creative and futuristic writing, both fiction and nonfiction, and are ahead of their time. Coming up with new ways to do things and thinking outside the box are parts of their skill set.

Loving to explore, most *1 Water* children go through life with a wide-eyed look on their face, observing and taking it all in. In Chinese medicine, water correlates with the kidneys and when out of balance can manifest as issues that affect the kidneys and related organs. The out-of-balance emotion is fear.

Clarity is needed to allow a *1 Water* person to move forward. Often *6 Metal* and *7 Metal* personalities are helpful in offering clarity for a *1 Water* person. *3 Tree* and *4 Tree* personalities can help a *1 Water* person in implementing new ways to express their ideas. When in balance, the water personality serves to help the metal personalities to decompress, and offers inspiration for their *3* and *4 Tree* friends. I will offer insights into a few *1 Water* personalities and discuss their inner and outer natures before I go on to the next personality type.

LAURA INGRAHAM

The 1 WATER, 4 TREE Personality
The Wave /The Wind

Philosophical, Active mind, Visionary, Creative, Cultural, Educator, Curious, Loves to learn, Sensitive, Love's forward movement.

Laura can appear very easy going and intellectually informed one minute, while the next she can have the effect of a large wave or the power of a gale-force wind.

Laura Ingraham, a *1 Water, 4 Tree*, appears tough and hard hitting on political topics. Her *4 Tree* nature is pragmatic, tenacious, and smart. She is great at picking things apart to show the big picture and the inconsistencies in politics. Her *1 Water* nature is visionary, creative, and free flowing and her matter-of-fact approach appeals to both men and women.

People she trusts and is close to would most likely say she wears her heart on her sleeve and is a sensitive person, which is depicted in her *1 Water, 4 Tree* nature. Her home life is a life learning experience for her, and she should be open to learning from and with her children, as well as realizing that every relationship offers teaching moments for all of those involved.

Radio fits the *1 Water* expression and is a perfect platform for her to use her intellectual *4 Tree* nature to verbalize, discuss, have dialog, express insights, and educate the public about the *1 Water* bigger picture at hand.

She offers common sense and can articulate intellectually stimulating ideas. Her *4 Tree* nature sees irony and a cultural decline that she cannot help but point out. Her sense of humor about life and her curiosity to know what makes people tick shows up on her Life Zette website. Here, she gets to be in a more relaxed venue, which is perfect for her to balance and support both sides of her nature: her *1 Water* free-flowing nature and her *4 Tree* philosophical nature.

She is a *1 Water* observer and her *4 Tree* analytic mind sees clearly the cause and effect of what is happening in today's world. The seeds that are planted produce the fruit that shapes the future; she educates her listeners about this advancing narrative that she sees as dysfunctional and destructive.

Laura's *1 Water, 4 Tree* nature serves as a voice that cuts to the chase and is able to discuss Donald Trump's Message. She is passionate about her beliefs, her family, and the country. Her *4 Tree* nature is why she is always meticulous about speech, composition, and sentence structure.

Being a speechwriter would be a great job for her, and she was one in the Reagan administration. This job allowed her to express a *1 Water* vision, while her *4 Tree* nature ensured the composition was perfect. She needs people around her to stay in sync with all her ideas and goals.

I will now share with you two *1 Water* Personalities that ran for president in recent elections. **Mitt Romney**, *8 Earth, 1 Water* and **John McCain**, *1 Water, 2 Earth*. You can read about the *2 Earth* personality next in the *2 Earth* section, and the *8 Earth* personality later in the book.

Together with **Hillary Clinton**, no matter how hard they try they do not have the Charismatic *9 Fire* personality. Thus, a "yes, we can" message did not work for them, though for different reasons. All three lacked clarity while running for office. All three candidates have personalities where their outer natures conflict with, fight against, or override their inner natures. So, they appear disjointed, confused, and seem awkward at best.

They are not resolved within themselves, and that clearly sticks out like a sore thumb. Combine the lack of *9 Fire* charisma with a wet blanket message results in a less-than-ideal candidate. I will discuss **John McCain** and **Mitt Romney** next. They are both *1 Water* personalities. I will discuss Hillary's personality later in the book. Their failures as

candidates do not mean that their skill sets could
not be useful and beneficial in other circumstances.

JOHN MCCAIN

The 1 WATER, 2 EARTH Personality
The Wave/ The Expressive

John McCain spends his time bouncing back and forth, struggling with the two natures in his personality, often without clarity. His *1 Water* nature is free flowing, expansive, and wants to understand the global big picture. His inner, *2 Earth* nature is shaped by his relationships with others, always cares about what others think, and wants consensus. He is detailed and wants to gather all the information possible to make a decision.

A *1 Water* nature is focused on the big picture, interested in expansion, and considers how decisions that are made today will affect the future. McCain's tendency is to have an inner push-pull conflict; he constantly overrides and curtails his *1 Water* expansive nature to meet the *2 Earth* needs of the group.

Since McCain's **2 Earth** nature is driven emotionally to connect to others and reach out to be in a relationship, he strives to reach the middle and agree. Two is better than one and more than two is even better for passing a bill through give-and-take consensus. His energy bounces back and forth, trying to see how to compromise to meet his needs.

McCain is passionate about the military. He has clarity on that subject because he has gained respect as an authority who can speak about or give an opinion on military matters.

Otherwise, he appears as a limp fish and wishy-washy. Note that I said appears; this does not mean John McCain does not have great ideas or good intentions. It does mean that he always has an inner fight on how best to handle things.

Who did he pick as a running mate? **Sarah Palin**, who is a **9 Fire** personality who loves the limelight and has charisma, whether you like her or not. She is a firecracker and the media sought to take the wind out of her sails before she could even get going. Furthermore, she made John McCain look even more like a limp fish like because she is a larger-than-life character.

Senator *Jeff Flake*, another similar personality, *2 Earth, 1 Water*, has been on talk shows expressing his *2 Earth* version of his idea of "The Story" of what a conservative is supposed to be. I respect that he wants to share his views, but I wonder to whom he is talking. He is not talking to the people of the United States, who are not happy with the wishy-washy approach that he is describing as the proper political etiquette of his version of being a conservative. If he would like to help America, he should move aside and let someone take his position of power so they can help the country. Why not get to work for the people?

MITT ROMNEY

The 8 EARTH, 1 WATER Personality
The Introspect/ The Wave

Mitt Romney has similar issues as John McCain, but, unlike McCain, he is not driven towards constant consensus in the sense that it does not define how he makes decisions. Mitt Romney's surface **8 Earth** personality is detailed and controlled. He is very businesslike, refined, family first, and can seem a bit austere. His strong faith is up front and guides him. His inner **1 Water** nature is the opposite: he is inventive, expansive, and free flowing, which is not at all like his outer nature.

So, one side of his nature must give in to the other, except when clarity is interjected. A strong purpose that meets the criteria of both sides of his nature and bridges the push pull within him is needed to create balance and a clear direction.

As governor of Massachusetts, his **8 Earth** nature wanted to stick to the budget, but his **1 Water** nature was always drawn to expansion, as is

depicted in his healthcare plan. His nature was to expand and create new programs while, at the same time, his detailed **8 Earth** nature was cautious and businesslike. Running for president must not have been easy for him. Although he had many good ideas and good intentions, he appeared disengaged and removed. He was described in the media as contradictory because within himself he was.

Even the people who worked for him in his businesses shared how they felt and how great he was to work for. Many saw him as a fabulous person, but that could not change how he came off to the public. He always seemed to struggle presenting a clear purpose. Along with that, he lacks **9 Fire** Charisma.

The 2 EARTH Personality

The Expressive

There are 3 *Earth* personalities: the *2 Earth*, the *5 Earth*, and the *8 Earth*.

The *2 Earth* personality is outgoing, chatty, enjoy sharing their feelings and being a good listener. *2 Earth* personalities define life by the relationships they have with those around them. Emotion exudes from *2 Earth* personalities. If they are telling a story, they add every detail along with everything they were feeling at the time.

The audience of a *2 Earth* speaker must listen very carefully to get through from start to finish without glazing over a bit. It is natural for a *2 Earth* to join a club, be a part of a group, and be attracted to team efforts. The *2 Earth* personality can also be the person going into the military.

Quick to offer their opinion, they want to know what everyone feels and thinks. They have mastery over and a love of telling "the story," with all its bells and whistles. *2 Earth* people use facial expressions, arm movements, and tone in their voice to express the point. They can be very loving people, wanting to help in any way they can. However, at the same time, they can appear bossy and demanding to those that really do not want their opinion.

Many people in the media that are the *2 Earth* personality are very expressive and seem to act out the emotion related to the topic at hand. Martha Raddatz, *2 Earth, 2 Earth*, seems to weep through her news reports, anxious and alarmed. Her voice and facial expressions are directly expressed.

Emotion is how they navigate the world. They are detailed and love to gather information. They want to be around people: it is what gives them energy. For those who are not chatty and want just the minimum amount of information, a *2 Earth* person can be draining. Emotion is the tool a *2 Earth* uses

to invoke a reaction; they use emotion and feelings
to navigate the world.

In politics, you often see the team of **Mary Matalin,
*2 Earth, 5 Earth***, and **James Carville, *2 Earth,
3 Tree***, on talk shows. They have had decades-long
careers as political consultants. They debate and
offer opposing sides of politics. I have always
thought they must hate each other in real life.
Actually, they are perfect together once I looked up
their personality types. Mary and James play off
each other so well; it is a real show.

Both are *2 Earth* personalities who love debating
the emotional story of what is happening on both
sides of the aisle. This manifests very differently in
each, but they both put forth concerns and emotions
about the divide between the left and the right.

James Carville is a *2 Earth, 3 Tree*. He appears
snarky, mildly obnoxious, insulting, and his voice
often sounds condescending. That is his *3 Tree* side
that knows he can be overtly over the top. This is
balanced out by Mary, with a point of view that is

more reasonable and authoritative, as expressed by her **5 Earth** nature. She is a **2 Earth, 5 Earth**. She appears sensible and knowledgeable. Her **5 Earth** personality has the ability to share the facts and be comfortable being his counter partner.

He uses his divisive attitude to get a rise out of the listener and to make people get worked up, even when he knows that what he is saying may be half-truths or not true at all. He is masterful at the art of throwing out conflict and controversy and seeing what sticks.

After he has expressed his agenda-based rhetoric like granny being thrown under the bus, Matalin serves as the balance by offering the other side of the same topic. They know that he has to act unglued to be entertaining and keep people's attention, even if he infuriates the listener. I always thought she must want to tell him to shut up, but that is why they have made a successful business out of combative dialog. They are masterful at focusing on the emotion of "the story".

Paul Begala, who acts similarly, is the same
personality type, but his outer nature is *3 Tree* and
inner is *2 Earth*. Both express themselves in the
same condescending snarky way. This is why they
are paid to offer their opinion: they say it like it is,
with no filter.

2 EARTH PERSONALITIES

	Outer Nature	**Inner Nature**
Chuck Schumer	5 Earth	2 Earth
Ted Kennedy	5 Earth	2 Earth
Cecilia Vega	5 Earth	2 Earth
Elizabeth Vargus	2 Earth	5 Earth
Kathie Lee Gifford	2 Earth	5 Earth
Meredith Vieira	2 Earth	1 Water
Savannah Guthrie	2 Earth	1 Water
Bill Ayers	2 Earth	1 Water
Alan Greenspan	2 Earth	1 Water
Jeff Flake	2 Earth	1 Water
John McCain	1 Water	2 Earth
Martha Raddatz	2 Earth	2 Earth
Carl Bernstein	2 Earth	2 Earth
Dick Durbin	2 Earth	2 Earth
Jeb Bush	2 Earth	2 Earth

Sally Jessy Raphael	2 Earth	2 Earth
Oprah	2 Earth	9 Fire
Saul Alinsky	2 Earth	9 Fire
Jim Acosta	2 Earth	9 Fire
F Roosevelt	2 Earth	9 Fire
Ginger Zee	2 Earth	9 Fire
Brian Kilmeade	9 Fire	2 Earth
John Kasich	3 Tree	2 Earth
D Eisenhower	2 Earth	3 Tree
Lyndon Johnson	2 Earth	5 Earth
John Kennedy	2 Earth	8 Earth
Marilyn Monroe	2 Earth	8 Earth
Rudy Giuliani	2 Earth	8 Earth
Tony Blair	2 Earth	8 Earth
Ronald Reagan	8 Earth	2 Earth
Anderson Cooper	6 Metal	2 Earth
Roger Ailes	6 Metal	2 Earth
H. R. McMaster	2 Earth	6 Metal
Robert Mueller	2 Earth	6 Metal
Julian Assange	2 Earth	7 Metal
George Soros	7 Metal	2 Earth

Marilyn Monroe and **John Kennedy** both had their
2 Earth "Story" out in the open. The Kennedy family
was always up and out in the limelight and their
story pulled at the public's heartstrings. Marilyn's
emotional up-and-down roller coaster ride played
out on the big screen. This is opposed to **Ronald
Reagan**; his outer *8 Earth* nature was reserved and
heartfelt, while his inner *2 Earth* nature was the
part of his personality visible in a speech, but it was
not front and center.

 Julian Assange, *2 Earth, 7 Metal*, and **George
Soros**, *7 Metal, 2 Earth*, both played a huge role in
the 2016 presidential campaign. Both have the
7 metal nature that systematically and successfully
saturated the media.

George Soros saturated the left with funds to
support and shape the Democratic platform. His
group hired people to riot and push his *2 Earth*
Story, strategically emphasizing a group victimhood
mentality. Julian Assange, *2 Earth, 7 Metal*, through
Wikileaks, exposed many of the emails and motives

that showed the "Storyline" of how Democrats sabotaged Bernie Sanders right out of the running. Julian Assange also let people see what goes on behind the scenes to control the masses.

John Kasich, *3 Tree, 2 Earth*, spent a lot of time in the presidential primaries pulling at the heartstrings of Americans with the "Story," a *2 Earth* approach to running for president. His *3 Tree* nature was front and center in a firm, thunderous way of telling it like he saw it on topics. Then, he would fall into a *2 Earth* story, where all the emotion would weep out with accompanying facial expressions. The *2 Earth* personality type, like that of like John McCain, tends to want group consensus and approval, and cares about the relationship factor of politics.

His *3 Tree* nature, however, could care less about what others think. So, a push pull conflict exists between the *3 Tree* and *2 Earth* regarding group consensuses: a very hard place to be in politics. Many voters felt he supported individuals' rights to be themselves, and was concerned about fiscally conservative principles. He is a personality type that wants to try new things, expansion, and growth. A push pull exists within, because on some issues he would tend to have one side win out over the other.

OPRAH WINFREY and SAUL ALINSKY

The 2 EARTH, 9 FIRE Personality
The Expressive/ The Flamboyant

MEDIA and DRAMA
Masters at crafting "The Story"

Media Mogul Oprah Winfrey created a platform for people to openly express their feelings. She loves the *9 Fire* limelight. Creating her own media conglomerate gave her many ways to reach the masses. Anyone could come on her daytime TV show and tell his or her story. Her guests could confess that they never stayed on their diet, or that they are gay or have been molested; they could express on TV anything that they wanted to. The more suffering it caused them the better. They would tell stories about how the past messed them up or explain why they are the way they are. This is the detailed *2 Earth* "Story." Using this story was how Oprah related to her listeners, and how they related to her.

9 Fire passion and charisma combined with a provoking *2 Earth* emotional trauma can create a drawn out painful story. This is the Drama that often plays out on today's reality TV shows.

This also plays out on the news in the morning, on most talk shows, and on social media, which is the perfect playground for slinging emotional baggage. Oprah started that train along with **Phil Donahue**, *2 Earth, 1 Water*, another *2 Earth* personality. It has now become the normal approach to broadcasting and journalism. Soap operas have nothing on the news or politics today.

Both Oprah and Phil are *2 Earth* personalities. They know "It is all about the story." **Sally Jessy Raphael**, another *2 Earth, 2 Earth* personality, was front and center in the mainstream at the time. Emotion-based "The Story" talk shows led the way.

It seems that respect for others takes a back burner today. We do not stand up, plain and simple, and say it is not acceptable to riot, ruin people's property, and steal from others. We have created a monster morality, and "I deserve to have what you have" mentality.

One way this has happened is by giving credence to reality TV and watching shows about a bachelor picking a wife from random sultry women who have been told who to be and how to sell "The Story." But why stop there?; the news today has become drama as well. **David Muir**, *9 Fire, 5 Earth*, on ABC dramatically shapes the storyline. Often political news headlines the first sensational story, then is followed by human interest stories designed to play on the viewers emotions, provoking lots of drama but nothing of real substance.

Where is the News? **Martha Raddatz** cries with much emotion and gasping as she shares the news, because it is "the story." When has it served the public to have the news acted out?

She is a *2 Earth, 2 Earth*, so she lacks the *9 Fire* charisma personality of Oprah, but she still has the

2 Earth expressive facial expressions to say it all.
She emotionally sells a story and it does not matter
if she believes it or not.

The world we live in today is no more than a tabloid
story. My goal is to point out the personality types
that affect what we see on TV. Oprah and Saul
Alinsky, both influential *2 Earth, 9 Fire* charismatic
personalities, used pain and suffering to capitalize
on emotions to influence the world. Find an
emotional pain trigger and push that button and
you have a new reality show. Housewives go mad;
loot your way to success, creating an endless loop of
feeling it's alright to be unaccountable for your own
actions.

Yes, politics is also directly in the world of emotions.
Chuck Schumer, *5 Earth, 2 Earth*, shouts from the
roof tops, "People will die," so you must pay more
money for health plans to save them. OK, Chuck,
fork over your millions; you can use your money
and throw that into the pot. My point is that
whatever political side you are on, we do not need a

"Drama and Reality Show" mentality influencing what shapes our world.

WIKIPEDIA's description of Oprah

"Dubbed the 'Queen of All Media,' she has been ranked the richest African-American, the greatest black philanthropist in American history, and is currently North America's first and only multi-billionaire black person. Several assessments rank her as the most influential woman in the world.

Winfrey was born into poverty in rural Mississippi to a teenage single mother and later raised in an inner-city Milwaukee neighborhood. She has stated that she was molested during her childhood and early teens and became pregnant at 14; her son died in infancy. Sent to live with the man she calls her father, a barber in Tennessee, Winfrey landed a job in radio while still in high school and began co-anchoring the local evening news at the age of 19.

Her emotional ad-lib delivery eventually got her transferred to the daytime talk show arena, and after boosting a third-rated local Chicago talk show to first place, she launched her own production company and became internationally syndicated.

Credited with creating a more intimate confessional form of media communication, she is thought to have popularized and revolutionized the tabloid talk show genre pioneered by Phil Donahue which a Yale study says broke 20th century taboos and allowed LGBT people to enter the mainstream."

If you read closely, you can see that every sentence is rich in the emotion of the *2 Earth.* "The Story," which is all about the confessional and tabloid form of media that exists today. This has a polarizing effect on society. Ayn Rand would probably tell Atlas it is time to shrug.

SAUL ALINSKY, BARACK OBAMA'S and HILLARY CLINTON'S mentor

I am not so sure why anyone would like what Saul Alinsky, *2 Earth, 9 Fire*, stood for, but I can certainly see how the tools that he used and mastered for controlling the masses are now used by the media and became a guide for winning the presidency in 2008. He has had a powerful influence in our politics and how the media has treated Donald Trump since he became president. **Saul Alinsky** mastered the Fake News approach, keeping your opponent off balance always defending his or her position. His famous quotes include,

"Restructure society, all life is warfare."

"Rub raw the sores of discontent."

"Whenever possible, go outside the expertise of the enemy. Look for ways to increase insecurity, anxiety, and uncertainty."

*"Pick the target, freeze it, personalize it, and polarize
it."*

*"Cut off the support network and isolate the target
from sympathy. Go after people and not institutions;
people hurt faster than institutions."*

Saul Alinsky was an all-purpose activist who knew
community organizing was a craft, a cunning and
true art for manipulating the masses.

TWO SHAPERS OF SOCIETY

I am not saying Oprah did not have pain or suffering in her life. I am not saying anything negative about her original intentions. I am saying that she used her experience as a black woman who had pain and suffering in her life to create an empire. She used the **9 Fire** dramatic, "Yes We Can" flair along with the **2 Earth** emotional telling of a story.

A sad story evokes emotion. If puppies are involved, that is even better. Jared Kushner has the same ability to be a shaper of society. Other **9 Fire, 2 Earth** personalities include Jim Acosta and Rand Paul. Whether you like them or not, they influence the public by pushing emotional buttons on TV news, in politics, and in social media. If used for the right reasons and with a sincere motive, **9 Fire, 2 Earth** is a powerful combination.

ALAN GREENSPAN

The 2 EARTH, 1 WATER Personality
The Expressive/ The Wave

Alan Greenspan served five terms as chairman of the Board of Governors of the Federal Reserve System. He originally took office as chairman on August 11, 1987 to fill an unexpired term as a member of the Board of Governors. His last term ended on January 31, 2006. He was appointed chairman by four different presidents.

Greenspan had many fans and many critics. He was a friend of Ayn Rand and followed her philosophy of Objectivism. She offered solutions to both sides of his nature.

I remember watching him on TV making his forecasts and sharing his thoughts. He often seemed to struggle, feel torn, continually compromising between two different ways of looking at the concerns at the time.

After going off the gold standard, he was quoted as saying he thought the US did extremely well without a central bank and with a gold standard. This change seemed outside his comfort zone. Besides that, people were held prisoner by the Federal Reserve's actions. This was a very tumultuous time, and the push pull within him played out for the public to see.

He "responded to his critics... defended his ideology as applied to his conceptual and policy framework, which, among other things, prohibited him from exerting real pressure against the burgeoning housing bubble or, in his words, 'leaning against the wind.'" Greenspan argued, "My view of the range of dispersion of outcomes has been shaken, but not my judgment that free competitive markets are by far the unrivaled way to organize economies." He concluded, "We have tried regulation ranging from heavy to central planning. None meaningfully worked. Do we wish to retest the evidence?"

One of his critics called him a "classic con man" who, through political savvy, "flattered and bullshitted his way up the Matterhorn of American power."

His *2 Earth* nature continually focused on being
frugal, practical, and fiscally responsible. When all
hell broke loose in the stock and housing market,
Alan Greenspan sat in the middle and had to
navigate the volatility and try to explain "The Story"
playing out in our nation. It was clear he was torn
between regulations being restrictive or necessary
as the events played out.

His *1 Water* nature would want to be more
expansive, with less regulation. His *2 Earth* nature
would have struggled with ways to create stability,
fix the problem, and add structure. Balance is
always an earth/water struggle, especially when it
comes to money.

The 3 TREE Personality

The Thunderous

The next Trigram in the *I Ching* is **Thunder**. **Thunder** is the sound caused by lightning. Depending on the distance and nature of the lightning, **Thunder** can range from a sharp, loud crack to a long, low rumble. The sudden increase in pressure and temperature from lightning produces rapid expansion of the air around and within a bolt of lightning.

The Greek philosopher Aristotle, in the fourth century BC, speculated that thunder was caused by the collision of clouds. When a storm is coming, lightning strikes and thunder booms loudly and directly. The *3 Tree* personality often speaks before thinking about how the information will be received. This is similar to children saying it like it is, without a filter. It is refreshing to know exactly what they think and feel, but sometimes they unknowingly hurt people's feelings.

3 Tree personalities do not have the time to soften the message because, to them, that does not serve anyone. They are not being mean; just like thunder, they are direct and up front before moving to the next topic. "Get out of my way, I am coming through." The *3 Tree* personality can shake up things that is for sure. My neighbor, *3 Tree, 4 Tree*, came over to see my new Alexa, Amazon Echo. She heard me asking Alexa to find a Radio station to no avail. The first thing she did was say in a stern voice, "Alexa, Listen to me." Alexa said back, "I am listening to you." We all laughed: a true, *3 Tree* approach to Alexa.

Like a child, the *3 Tree* moves quickly from one thing to the next, trying new things and juggling lots of activities. Many *3 Tree* people need someone to follow behind them, keeping things moving in sync and reminding them that they have too many things going on. It is not that they cannot take care of themselves; they are just more able to keep all the balls in the air if someone is assisting them, lining up the schedule and catching the balls as they fly through the air.

The *3 Tree* personality manifests in different ways depending on the combination with the person's other personality type. My dad Dirty George, the same personality as Sean Hannity, was always on the go. There was never a dull moment. I am betting that Sean Hannity's team are very good jugglers; after all, he has a lot going on in every moment.

My dad had no problem being true to who he was and letting others know just what they need to do. He took good care of his employees and his family, although he embarrassed all of us on a regular basis. Everything he did or said had potential to be embarrassing, not because he was being unsavory, but because he did not have a filter. He never hesitated to call someone a fat head or a clown if they were not living up to their potential.

3 TREE PERSONALITIES

	Outer nature	Inner nature
Ted Cruz	3 Tree	4 Tree
Sean Hannity	3 Tree	4 Tree

Shannon Bream	3 Tree	4 Tree
Sam Donaldson	3 Tree	4 Tree
John Hancock	3 Tree	3 Tree
Dinesh D'Souza	3 Tree	3 Tree
Melania Trump	3 Tree	3 Tree
Jesse Waters	4 Tree	3 Tree
Willard Scott	3 Tree	4 Tree
Bob Woodward	3 Tree	4 Tree
Margaret Thatcher	3 Tree	6 Metal
Michelle Malkin	3 Tree	6 Metal
Sebastian Gorka	3 Tree	6 Metal
Johnny Carson	3 Tree	6 Metal
Ayn Rand	6 Metal	3 Tree
Larry Arnn	3 Tree	7 Metal
Patrick Henry	3 Tree	2 Earth
Rex Tillerson	3 Tree	2 Earth
D Eisenhower	2 Earth	3 Tree
Steve Doocy	8 Earth	3 Tree
Chris Wallace	8 Earth	3 Tree
Pat Buchanan	8 Earth	3 Tree
Robert Lighthizer	8 Earth	3 Tree
Ben Franklin	8 Earth	3 Tree
Bill Bennett	3 Tree	1 Water
Newt Gingrich	3 Tree	1 Water
Geraldo Rivera	3 Tree	1 Water

Barbara Bush	3 Tree	1 Water
James Carville	2 Earth	3 Tree
Paul Begala	3 Tree	2 Earth
Martin Luther King	3 Tree	9 Fire
B. Obama	3 Tree	9 Fire
Bret Baier	3 Tree	9 Fire
Greg Jarrett	9 Fire	3 Tree
Ted Yoho	9 Fire	3 Tree
Megyn Kelly	3 Tree	5 Earth
G. Stephanopoulos	3 Tree	5 Earth
Allen West	3 Tree	5 Earth

Again, the combination of the inner nature and the outer nature makes all the difference in how the personality type is expressed.

Sebastian Gorka, **Michelle Malkin**, and **Margaret Thatcher**, share the *3 Tree, 6 Metal* combination. All three are hard core fighters for the causes they believed in. "The Iron Lady," is a fitting name for this personality type.

Pat Buchanan is a wonderful example of the calm

8 Earth personality when he is sharing his historical insights into politics. He knows all the players and he understands political dynamics.

His *3 Tree* nature comes roaring out when asked what he thinks about something. His *3 Tree* inner nature is not going to hold back from telling you how he sees it. He does not care about the delivery of the message. He will chuckle a bit, but has no reservation about predicting an outcome. He shares Benjamin Franklin's *8 Earth, 3 Tree* personality type. One of his quotes is below.

"They who can give up essential liberty to obtain a little temporary safety deserve neither liberty nor safety."

Steve Doocy, *8 Earth, 3 Tree*, and **Chris Wallace**, *8 Earth, 3 Tree*, have the same controlled manner of calm on the outside. Their inner thunderous *3 Tree* nature is very noticeable when they have an opinion on a topic. *8 Earth, 3 Tree* personalities must be passionate about the job they are in or they will be very unhappy. They have a push pull inside between their **Earth** nature of being frugal and practical and their **Tree** nature that is spontaneous and action oriented. One side usually wins out over the other at any given time.

Patrick Henry, another **3 Tree**, stood for Liberty, and was known for his statement:

"I know not what others may choose but, as for me, give me liberty or give me death."

Vladimir Putin is **3 Tree, 7 Metal**. The Metal nature makes him not only direct with his delivery, it also makes him intense and steely. The combination of **3 Tree** and **7 Metal** forms a very strong personality: Don't poke the bear. His personality does not work well with those that appear pompous or pushy. His nature is precise and systematic. He values those that offer insights and wants them to communicate their viewpoints in clear and non-combatant ways. I remember looking at Putin's face on TV when Obama was telling him what he should do and not do. Obama poked the bear.

The *3 Tree* natures they both share boomed into
each other, like two thunderclouds. They express
the *3 Tree* nature in different ways. Obama is a
3 Tree personality combined with a flamboyant
9 Fire inner nature; this can make him appear
haughty and arrogant. Putin's *7 Metal*, sword-
drawn inner nature and Obama's *9 Fire* inner
nature are like night and day. The combination of
the inner and outer natures can create very
different individuals. Obama loves the limelight;
Putin is all business and couldn't care less about
being in the limelight.

Ayn Rand is a *6 Metal, 3 Tree* personality. I will
touch on her in the *6 Metal* section, but the quotes
below express her *3 Tree* nature.

*"The smallest minority on earth is the individual.
Those who deny individual rights cannot claim to be
defenders of minorities."*

"The question isn't who is going to let me; it's who is going to stop me."

"I swear by my life and my love of it that I will never live for the sake of another man, nor ask another man to live for mine."

"A creative man is motivated by the desire to achieve, not by the desire to beat others."

-Ayn Rand, *Atlas Shrugged*

SEAN HANNITY AND ANN COULTER

The 3 TREE, 4 TREE Personality
The Thunderous/ The Wind

Direct, Tells it like it is, Active mind, A fighter, Controversial, Love the facts, Bored easily, No nonsense, Spontaneous, Adventurous.

The personality type *3 Tree, 4 Tree* is like a Jack Russell Terrier pulling at your pant leg. These people have big voices and keep their eye on the ball, barking out their truth. *Thunder* is their Trigram in the *I Ching*. "Just give me the facts." Often, this personality speaks before thinking about the delivery. They love to tease those around them.

Coulter and Hannity are *3 Tree, 4 Tree* personalities. They are naturally curious and interested to learn new things. Both have the perfect venues to express their personalities. Ann's book writing and Sean's Radio and TV shows serve as perfect outlets for them to be the Truth seekers they are.

Many people say that *3 Tree, 4 Tree* people have the propensity to talk over others or can be extremely opinionated. *3 Tree, 4 Tree* individuals give a buffalo's behind about what anyone thinks about their political beliefs because they know in their heart they are what they are and have the facts to back it up. They do not like to have someone piss on their foot and say it is raining. This means they do not tolerate people who are full of BS and they admire anyone who stands up for what they believe.

Hannity and Coulter both got on the Trump train. They saw the need for an outsider and appreciated President Trump's *9 Fire*, larger-than-life personality: a force to be reckoned with. Both saw the now-or-never urgency for getting changes to happen. Their *4 Tree* natures are philosophical and search for expansive solutions, so Trump's business sense was appealing.

Close family members to Hannity and Coulter most likely roll their eyes at times and feel embarrassed by the *3 Tree, 4 Tree* candor and need to keep things in motion. The *3 Tree* attitude of "Time is money" and "Hurry up will YA" combines with the

4 Tree search for answers. These people are educated and on topic about the things they see value in.

These two *3 Tree* beacons, or maybe foghorns, for freedom bellow through the night, serving the warrior cause by being upfront about who they are. Urgency and candor are important in our political environment.

Ted Cruz, *3 Tree, 4 Tree*, is also this personality type. He is one of the few politicians that is there to serve the common good and call a spade a spade, fighting for the people. Cruz is another person, like Hannity, who other politicians would like to "Vote off the Island." We have spent so long with unproductive personality types in the political arena being old and stagnant on both sides of the isle. These politicians are murky swampers, limp fish types, and attention seekers who are full of bull.

Dinesh D'Souza, *3 Tree, 3 Tree*, and others so eloquently expose how they use their positions as a way of increasing their incomes and gaining power.

All the resistance on the left and right and the fabricated, fear-mongering, "throw granny off the train" rhetoric serves no one and devalues the person speaking such things. Politicians in general, on the right and the left, are elected and are funded by taxpayers. I think they forgot they work for us.

NEWT GINGRICH

The 3 TREE, 1 WATER Personality
The Thunderous/ The Wave

Says it like it is, Gift for writing, Ahead of the times, No nonsense thinker, Matter of fact, Sees the bigger picture, Educator, Historian, Good with numbers, Creative, Visionary, Futuristic.

Newt Gingrich, *3 Tree*, is similar to Sean Hannity, *3 Tree*, in the way he expresses himself in the world. Like Hannity, he strongly expresses his opinion, but the two are very different in their inner personalities. Gingrich is a *3 Tree* firecracker and a hard liner in his delivery, but his inner *1 Water* nature is free-flowing, futuristic, and speaks his truth calmly and succinctly.

Hannity has a *4 Tree* inner nature, which tends to speak in talking points, be on a quest for knowledge, and present the facts. The two men can deliver similar messages, but they do this in completely different ways. Gingrich has a flow to his messages and speaks in a calm, strong, monotone way.

Hannity has excitement in his voice, even when just listing the facts. Gingrich, however, often gives history lessons when presenting his messages.

When Gingrich is on Hannity's show, they gel very nicely and cover topics in a two-fisted way. Their *3 Tree* natures say it like it is. The phrase "A bull in the china closet" fits both men perfectly. Hannity has a more philosophical *4 Tree* nature while Newt, more expansive in his delivery, has a *1 Water* nature.

Sean Hannity has the *3 Tree* fog-horn approach to staying on message and supporting his narrative. Gingrich, like Hannity, supports the president and sees his value and vision. Gingrich is a *1 Water* big thinker, a visionary who is ahead of his time and shares Trump's inner nature. He is always playing chess and trying to broaden the playing field. Putting it differently, he is riding the wave, which often comes with uncertainty. Gingrich is a controversial figure, for sure.

Newt Gingrich serves as a great voice for sharing the history of what works and what does not work. His *3 Tree, 1 Water* nature offers practicality and the tools to fix problems; after all, he has first-hand experience. Hannity and Gingrich share a forward-thinking attitude, but Hannity, *3 Tree, 4 Tree*, is more in your face, and says, "Here is a list of what works, now do it."

Here is a perfect quote in the *Washington Post* from years ago. It shows Gingrich's outer personality and inner nature.

"Gingrich combines qualities rarely found in one politician: He is a brilliant speaker and debater, he is an effective (*3 Tree*) guerrilla on the House floor, and he is a genuine political strategist and theorist (*1 Water*), who by the force of his ideas has begun to reshape Republican politics. (*1 Water nature*)"

-David Broder of *The Washington Post*

Here is another quote about Gingrich from the same article:

"What stands out as particularly unique, however, is his fascination with "the future."

These quotes are a perfect description of the *1 Water* personality type.

There is also a plethora of negative stories and articles written over the past years saying that Gingrich is combative, controversial, a bad listener, forced his opinion on everyone, and threw everyone under the bus and ran over them as many times as he could. Many *New York Times* stories written over the years treated him as a person who needed to be taken out, come hell or high water. But *3 Tree* personalities do not stop, even if others "vote them off the island."

Bill Bennett, 3 Tree, 1 Water, shares the same personality type and has no problem telling it like it is He also has a very expansive view, both of past events and what he sees for the future.

SEBASTIAN GORKA

The 3 TREE, 6 METAL Personality
The Thunderous/ The Conduit

Piercing, Direct, Bulldog, Intense, Hates spin, Exposes intention, Fights for the truth, Brass tacks, Intuitive, Calls a spade a spade, Witty, Quick mind.

Sebastian Gorka has a combination of Sean Hannity's *3 Tree* nature and Kellyanne Conway's *6 Metal* nature. Though not in appearance, he shares Sean Hannity's willingness to take on fights and be a *3 Tree* bulldog who boxes with the those who continue to be deleterious to the Trump administration. Always with the goal in mind, Gorka controls conversations and *3 Tree* bulldogs his way to his point. When a *CNN* host was interviewing him, he did not allow her to take control of the narrative and told her *CNN*'s ratings were behind those of *Nick at Night*, cartoons, and Brady bunch reruns. His *3 Tree* nature hammers on the facts and his truth until the subject changes. He is despised by his opponents because he takes no prisoners.

Gorka shares Conway's **6 Metal** emotional nature; he is intuitive and able to sword fight with the best of them. With sword in hand, he can expose the person he is being interviewed by as misinformed and lacking in moral fiber. Getting things done fits his **6 Metal** nature and supports what Trump went to Washington to do.

Resistance and sabotage needs to be fought against with clarity and a vision in mind. Gorka's approach is: "If you want to have a constructive conversation and want to hear about what is going on, I am in. If you want to be adversarial and manipulate the conversation, then I will use your own game against you." People either love him or want to take him down, there is nothing in between.

Conway and Gorka's **6 Metal** natures are not the type to sit still while being asked stupid, misleading questions. They will expose people for their intentions.

Gorka supports both President Trump's visionary *1 Water* side and his *say-it-like-he-sees-it* *9 Fire* side. Gorka needs a reason to fight for a cause; he will not simply pick any topic to make a buck or be in the limelight.

Gorka's personality type is intense. Anyone who shares his *3 Tree, 6 Metal* personality type could use a walk by the sea to recharge and let their mind rest. Water and free-flowing activities are very good for this personality type.

The upward expanding *3 Tree* nature is very different from his contracting *6 Metal* nature. Both are fast moving, but they go in opposite directions. A push pull can occur within the *Metal/Tree* personality.

The 4 TREE Personality

The Wind

The next Trigram in the *I Ching* is the "WIND." Planting seeds and watching them grow, Wind occurs on a range of scales: from thunderstorm flows lasting tens of minutes, to local breezes generated by heating of land surfaces lasting a few hours, to global winds resulting from the difference in absorption of solar energy between the climate zones on Earth.

The wind is what carries and spreads seeds to faraway places. The wind spans the globe. *4 Tree* personalities are philosophical, love to learn, and love traveling the world and learning about different cultures. They are on a continual quest to broaden their horizons; they might be considered eternal learners.

Often, *4 Tree* individuals go into professions like Teaching and Law, and they make good presenters.

4 Trees are always looking for new ideas and enjoy new activities. They often are the first to look up what Wikipedia says about something they do not know about. They can get bored easily once they feel they have mastered something and quickly go to try something new. *4 Trees* make good writers and correspondents.

These individuals focus on what is going on around them and have a keen eye for exposing injustices. Many *4 Tree* personalities are notable for offering their insights and opinions. They have compassionate hearts and are curious. Travel and studying cultures fascinate them.

Investigating, looking to see what may be hidden under rocks, makes them tick. Often, *4 Trees* make very good lawyers because they cross-examine with ease. Again, looking at the inner and outer personalities combined gives the most insight into this personality and how *4 Trees* express themselves.

These individuals can be a turbulent gale wind or a light breeze. Both *3 Tree* and *4 Tree* personalities are active in the sky, as depicted in the active movement of the wind and changing weather.

4 TREE PERSONALITIES

	Outer Nature	Inner Nature
Laura Ingraham	1 Water	4 Tree
G. Van Susteren	1 Water	4 Tree
Ben Carson	4 Tree	1 Water
Tucker Carlson	4 Tree	5 Earth
Jeanine Pirro	4 Tree	5 Earth
James Comey	4 Tree	7 Metal
K Guilfoyle	4 Tree	7 Metal
Joe Biden	4 Tree	8 Earth
M Bloomberg	4 Tree	8 Earth
Mitch McConnell	4 Tree	8 Earth
George Bush Sr.	4 Tree	4 Tree
Lara Spencer	4 Tree	4 Tree
Jesse Waters	4 Tree	3 Tree
Ann Coulter	3 Tree	4 Tree
Sean Hannity	3 Tree	4 Tree
Ted Cruz	3 Tree	4 Tree

Paul Ryan	4 Tree	6 Metal
Jason Chaffetz	6 Metal	4 Tree
James Madison	6 Metal	4 Tree
Rachel Maddow	9 Fire	4 Tree
Colin Powell	9 Fire	4 Tree
Bernie Sanders	5 Earth	4 Tree
Sean Spicer	2 Earth	4 Tree
Steve Scalise	8 Earth	4 Tree
John Jay	7 Metal	4 Tree

Greta Van Susteren, *1 Water, 4 Tree*, loves to learn, be curious, get to the bottom of things, and intelligently examine the situation. Her *1 Water* personality makes her appear more in the flow, easy going, and intellectual. Laura Ingraham is like Van Susteren in that she makes intellectual investigative observations. She combines her *4 Tree* Lawyer mind with her more creative, free-flowing *1 Water* nature. That side of her makes her a comfortable and naturally dynamic radio or TV host.

Someone like **Mitch McConnell** is torn between his expansive, ever-changing *4 Tree* nature and the need to collect more information before moving forward of his **8 Earth** nature. One side will always tend to override the other, so he often appears less than effective. He lacks resolve and leadership. On the one hand, he is optimistic for change, as depicted in his **4 Tree** nature; on the other hand, his **8 Earth** nature resists, wanting to take one step at a time and plodding along before totally committing to a plan. This is a paralyzing place to be.

Joe Biden in the Democrat party, **4 Tree, 8 Earth**, and **Michael Bloomberg**, **4 Tree, 8 Earth**, share the same struggle within. It is evident that they share a push pull within themselves. One side loves to accumulate wealth, so the messages they politically support contradict their platforms. This makes them ineffective leaders because they appear to live in one reality while asking others to live in another.

Senator Thom Tillis, **4 Tree, 2 Earth**, is another person who uses the **2 Earth** "Story" to say that "the people" are more concerned about preserving

Mueller's biased special Council lynch mob than getting behind the elected president who has a job to do for the people. It seems there is no concern for the people; this exposes the insincerity and motives of the people we put in office.

This is a deleterious position for our country, as well as sad that it has become all about self-interest groups that dictate what they want and say it is what the people want. That is the negative expression of the *2 Earth* "Story" line. This type of person appears to crave being in the lime light and moving ahead in the political hierarchy.

James Comey appears disjointed as well. His outer *4 Tree* nature is philosophical and intellectual. His *7 Metal* nature is intense, combative, and overrides his outer nature. This can give off the vibe that he is Dr. Jekyll and Mr. Hyde.

Sean Spicer is a great example of a *4 Tree* personality who feels a push pull. His *2 Earth* nature did not enjoy the media negativity in the press room. He would have loved being able to deliver the agenda for the day in an informative and educational way. Sword fighting with the media was not fun for him, and he most likely felt completely drained on a daily basis.

Colin Powell and **Rachel Maddow**, both *4 Tree*, *9 Fire*, need to be on stage and be philosophical about their positions. So, at times they can appear to feel they are above the masses, or arrogant. Being in the limelight is their platform for telling everyone how they feel. Their sensitive side is hidden from the world, but at the same time is acted out on TV and in Politics.

Jesse Waters, *4 Tree, 3 Tree*, is similar to Sean Hannity and Ann Coulter, both *3 Tree, 4 Tree*, but his *4 Tree* outer nature makes him appear more investigative and interested in interviewing his guests. His thunderous *3 Tree* nature is obvious, but his delivery is a bit different. All three, however, have the intent to expose the truth.

Bernie Sanders would be more openly opinionated and would enjoy being at the center of things due to his **5 Earth** nature. Even though he sounded crusty on the campaign trail, he drew people in by appearing informed and knowledgeable. You will read about the **5 Earth** personality on the next page.

The 5 EARTH Personality

The Center

The *5 Earth* personality likes to be in the center of things. This type gravitates to leadership positions, politics, being the head of corporations, or holding high positions in the government or Military.
5 Earth people make excellent teachers because they offer the details needed to understand a subject. They like the problem-solving aspects of being on a team where everyone brings their gathered information to the table to formulate a plan to move forward. Even when a *5 Earth* does not know something, they often appear as if they do.

They try to collect as much information as possible before moving forward. You can ask any of the *5 Earth* personality combinations about the best restaurant in town or any other subject that they are knowledgeable about, and they will know all the details. They are usually the best at Trivia, historical events, and the details that are needed to make informative decisions.

Sometimes though, if they do not have **Metal** in their personality type, they may not know when to stop collecting or when enough is enough. They continue collecting and collecting, piling up resources. A good secretary is then needed to move the train forward. **5 Earth** personalities are a great resource.

They are strong personalities, authoritative, and will argue their points to the end. They can be stubborn and like a pit bull in an argument. Many people find them entertaining, social, and fun to be around. Often, they will gravitate to the center of the party. They like to run the show.

5 EARTH PERSONALITIES

	Outer Nature	Inner Nature
A. Napolitano	5 Earth	7 Metal
Mike Pence	5 Earth	7 Metal
Rob Marciano	5 Earth	7 Metal
Mark Meadows	5 Earth	6 Metal
Bob Dole	5 Earth	6 Metal

Tom Cotton	5 Earth	8 Earth
Scott Pruitt	5 Earth	8 Earth
John Kelly	5 Earth	8 Earth
Henry Kissinger	5 Earth	8 Earth
John Boehner	6 Metal	5 Earth
Tim Kane	6 Metal	5 Earth
Barbara Boxer	6 Metal	5 Earth
Tom Brokaw	6 Metal	5 Earth
M Gorbachev	6 Metal	5 Earth
Dolley Madison	7 Metal	5 Earth
David Muir	9 Fire	5 Earth
Brian Williams	5 Earth	9 Fire
Winston Churchill	9 Fire	5 Earth
Glenn Beck	9 Fire	5 Earth
Jim Jordan	9 Fire	5 Earth
David Axelrod	9 Fire	5 Earth
Susan Rice	9 Fire	5 Earth
Rush Limbaugh	5 Earth	9 Fire
Eric Holder	5 Earth	9 Fire
Rick Perry	5 Earth	2 Earth
Cecilia Vega	5 Earth	2 Earth
Chuck Schumer	5 Earth	2 Earth
Ted Kennedy	5 Earth	2 Earth
Maxine Waters	8 Earth	5 Earth
Loretta Lynch	5 Earth	8 Earth

Lester Holt	5 Earth	1 Water
Joseph Stalin	5 Earth	1 Water
Charlie Rose	5 Earth	1 Water
Donna Brazile	5 Earth	1 Water
C Krauthammer	5 Earth	1 Water
Dana Perino	1 Water	5 Earth
Mike Wallace	1 Water	5 Earth
Megyn Kelly	3 Tree	5 Earth
Victoria Toensing	5 Earth	3 Tree
James Mattis	5 Earth	4 Tree
Jeanine Pirro	4 Tree	5 Earth
Tucker Carlson	4 Tree	5 Earth
Bernie Sanders	5 Earth	4 Tree
Al Franken	4 Tree	5 Earth

All are strong personalities who like to be in charge. They speak with authority and have no problem offering their opinions. Personalities with *5 Earth* as the outer personality take charge and love standing in the middle of things, like Bernie Sanders. His *4 Tree* side is more philosophical.

Dana Perino has the *1 Water* outer nature. She appears more easy going, but her strong, bold *5 Earth* personality type is very evident when she is sharing her opinion. *5 Earth* combined with *9 Fire* personality types enjoy being in the limelight in one way or another. They are entertaining and have charisma. *Brian Williams*, *5 Earth, 9 Fire*, and *David Muir*, *9 Fire, 5 Earth*, have a dramatic approach to the news.

Rush Limbaugh, *5 Earth, 9 Fire*, and *Glen Beck*, *9 Fire, 5 Earth*, share the Fire/Earth combination. The difference is Rush is outwardly a *5 Earth* personality, an informative and strong presence in talk radio. His *9 Fire* inward nature is the storyteller and he uses the charismatic *9 Fire* side of his nature to be entertaining and make him fun to listen to.

Glenn Beck is the opposite to Limbaugh. His outer nature is the more dramatic *9 Fire* storyteller. He enjoys attention and being acknowledged for his *5 Earth* advice and informative dialog. Glenn is dramatic, emotional, and expressive, and he shows his passion for the subject he is talking about. Limbaugh's *5 Earth* outer nature is more matter of fact, showing very little emotion and just stating observations. Both have been accused as coming off as "know-it-alls." Rush has no problem using his funny sense of humor to tell you he does, in fact, know it all.

In contrast, **Mike Wallace** and **Charles Krauthammer** are *5 Earths* who are more serious and share the *1 Water* personality. Both have an authoritative approach to expressing their opinion.

Megyn Kelly, *3 Tree, 5 Earth*, and **Victoria Toensing**, *5 Earth, 3 Tree*, are both lawyers with very strong personalities. These very vocal *3 Tree* individuals have no problem being in an in-charge position. Radio and TV are media outlets that serve to support their personalities. Kelly's thunderous *3 Tree* nature is what people saw during the presidential campaign. Toensing's *5 Earth* nature is what people see in her outer nature, so she puts forth a practical informative delivery. Her *3 Tree* nature is there, just not on the surface.

Keep in mind that an inner struggle exists in people that are Earth-Water or Tree-Earth because all 3 of the earth personalities are detailed and practical; they always consider the practicality of things.

These types tend to override the more spontaneous or free-flowing part of themselves.

Writers that are Earth and Water tend to write up a storm in a free-flowing *1 Water* nature way and then the *5 Earth* nature will over edit the material, often losing the free-flowing aspects that make a good piece to read.

RUSH LIMBAUGH

The 5 EARTH, 9 FIRE Personality
The Center/ The Flamboyant

Informative, Story Teller, Collector of information, Knows he offends people, Controversial, Opinionated, Authoritative, Historian, Kind, Knows his limitations, Big hearted, Loves to get a rise out people, Educator.

The original MEDIA WARRIOR. Limbaugh's *9 Fire* inner nature appreciates and loves Trump's ability to get out in the public and take the media to the cleaners. His *5 Earth* take-charge nature sees the value in a non-political figure doing a shake down of a system that has not served the public for years.

He is a strong, *5 Earth, 9 Fire* personality type and loves the radio platform, where he can be expressive and tell stories with deliberate analysis. Limbaugh's *5 Earth* nature offers informative, entertaining insights into the ways of politics, and he gladly pats himself on the back for his entertaining **9 Fire** analysis. He enjoys what he does and knows his limitations. Storytelling is a **9 Fire** gift he possesses. I love his historical, **5 Earth** factual children's books; they are fabulous and, politics aside, everyone should read them.

He uses his **9 Fire** side to entertain the reader with factual stories and teaches history by going back in time with Liberty the talking horse, a charismatic **9 Fire** type personality that loves attention. It is great bedtime reading.

Limbaugh, as a **5 Earth**, has an intimate connection to our history and lacks tolerance for those who want to blame others for their problems and insecurities. He is dedicated to educating the public about what has happened in the past and what is happening now and how it affects the future. Limbaugh knows his audience, though those on the left say he can be inflammatory. Remember, the **9 Fire** is a storyteller. Thomas Jefferson was also a **5 Earth, 9 Fire.**

"No nation ever taxed itself into prosperity"

*You know why there's a Second Amendment? In case
the government fails to follow the first one.*

-Rush Limbaugh

MARK STEYN

The 5 EARTH, 1 WATER Personality
The Center/ The Wave

Uses wit to show the truth, Authoritative, Excellent commentator, Writer, Historian, Entertainer, Free flowing, Visionary, Creative, In control.

Mark Steyn is a MEDIA warrior. He is a *5 Earth, 1 Water*. This type makes great researchers and collectors of information. In Steyn's case, he can use his vision and insights through his *1 Water* nature to show the big picture. Being a Radio host, writing, and singing are free-flowing ways of expressing himself. This comes naturally to the *1 Water* personality. Steyn uses his creativity and humor to state the facts in a *5 Earth* way. He speaks authoritatively, telling it as he sees it.

Mark Steyn is an effective Warrior. He utilizes both sides of his nature to educate and use his knowledge to honestly depict the state of affairs around the world.

He has charm and has a way of making everyone laugh because of the way he uses information to show how most of what you see in the news is not possibly true. One cannot help but giggle out loud when listening to him on the radio. He points out how, in general, we have been over regulated and we work to keep politicians fat and happy: they do not work for us.

Mark Steyn would not survive without his other part, full of *1 Water* song and fanfare, to balance his life. Hence, he lives in the state where I grew up, where the license plates say, "Live, freeze and die." OK, it's actually "Live free or Die." He is a Global beacon and a visionary. Paul Revere was the same personality type.
 "Sons of Liberty"

Any personality type that is Earth and Water struggles with being free flowing on the one hand and structured and detailed on the other hand. This means the struggle of the *5 Earth* practical frugal nature often overrides the free-flowing *1 Water* expansive nature. Steyn's media commentary combines and balances the 2 sides nicely.

MIKE PENCE

The 5 EARTH, 7 METAL Personality
The Center/ The Pragmatist

Likes being in the center, Informative, Social, Grounded, confident, Resolved, Intuitive, Strong personality, Collector of information. Appears calm on the outside, even when he does not feel that way.

Vice President Mike Pence's personality type is a great VP choice for President Donald Trump. The **5 Earth, 7 Metal** personality type's demeanor is calm and his mission is clear. This personality type feels negotiation is the best way to resolve differences, but will not hesitate to pull out the sword. They use facts and information to back up their inner knowledge.

5 Earth personalities are drawn to being in the political arena because they can be at the center of things, but also see where things need to go to be productive. They have the ability to articulate a message with ease and with composure. Do not make the *5 Earth, 7 Metal* personality type mad or heads will fall. The media and politicians better not be fooled by Mike Pence's calm demeanor. If he feels that someone is not being sincere, he will let them know. The *5 Earth* personality can appear stubborn and it is hard to change their minds.

The *5 Earth, 7 Metal* has a cannon. This means they will always take a gathering-the-posse approach to unite for a cause first, but will tire if there is no movement. Since Mike Pence has President Trump behind him as the president, he will fight for the removal of the "The Swamp", those that have too much power in politics and are not serving the common good of our citizens. Do not be surprised if mild-mannered Mike Pence, *5 Earth, 7 Metal*, brings out his cannon soon.

His *5 Earth, 7 Metal* personality offers President Trump insights into the political world and sincere support to getting things done for the forgotten man and, frankly, for all people. Many people said that Mike Pence was the safe choice for Donald Trump. No. Rather, he is the perfect *5 Earth, 7 Metal* personality choice. Remember, this is not about politics; it is all about personality types. It is also about the combination of *5 Earth* with *7 Metal* that makes up this personality type. A *5 Earth* personality combined with, say, a *3 Tree* would not have the same drive and intuition. The metal nature is a force that cuts through the weeds and, with sword drawn, marches forward.

JAMES MATTIS

The 5 EARTH, 4 TREE Personality
The Center/ The Wind

James Mattis has a take-charge, intellectual, and forceful personality. He was a very good choice for the president to pick for the position he holds.
5 Earth, 4 Tree personalities are authoritative and offer a philosophical approach to leadership. People gravitate to this type, as they are good at being in the center and in charge. *5 Earth* personalities love to collect information and, if combined with *4 Tree*, have a *4 Tree* worldly flair.

Mattis understands the playing field and needs a commander in chief that is strong and resolved. His *5 Earth, 4 Tree* nature does not take orders blindly. He would never take men or women into battle carelessly and without thought of the consequences.

He is a *5 Earth*, which makes him strong willed, but his emotional *4 Tree* nature is a good counter, so he would be well aware that the seeds he plants will affect the future. The media portrays him as a hard ass, but I think they miss the total picture.

He established the Center for Advanced Operational Culture Learning, a training academy for marine officers and senior enlisted personnel, to instill cultural awareness and language skills. He emphasized the "hearts and minds" approach to counterinsurgency operations. That is a *4 Tree* approach of respecting the cultural and the philosophical aspects needed in the war against terrorists.

Mattis is a *5 Earth* hard hitter, but also a *4 Tree*, sensitive to the hearts and minds of all that are involved. He seems to consider all aspects of cultural influence and views things with a holistic approach. If I did not know his personality type and just followed the news I would think "Maddog Mattis" was a brute force commander, but in reality that is not true. The *4 Tree* intellectual, strategic, and educated side combines with his forceful *5 Earth* resolve to make a good combination for his position.

Any person that is a *Tree* and *Earth* personality struggles with the 2 sides of their personality. The Earth is practical and detailed, but the Tree more spontaneous and quick to act. This results in a possible push pull.

The 6 METAL Personality
The Conduit

When we think of metal, we think of steel, gold, silver, copper, aluminum, brass, nickel, titanium, and others.

The *6 Metal* and *7 Metal* personalities are similar to an electrical capacitor. A capacitor is a vessel for storing energy. When it reaches its capacity, it releases a charge of electrical energy and fires a powerful spark. Electrical conductivity is a measure of a material's ability to conduct an electric current.

6 Metal individuals are like a train in motion, moving speedily to get to the goal at hand. The metal train track is a direct route to the destination. They love to complete things and cross things off their list. They are extremely creative, intense, and have very active minds. Like a capacitor, energy flows through them. The *6 Metal* personality is always looking for what can be done and then taking care of it. They take that approach both in their jobs and for their family members.

6 Metal people are very intuitive and can feel what others are feeling. They might not know why but they feel what is going on. They have a strong sense of responsibility and both *6* and *7 metal* personalities have leadership qualities. If they follow their very first gut feeling, they are usually right. Often, they will overthink and overanalyze, which tends to cause them to second-guess themselves.

They are decision makers and benefit from Earth personalities who love to collect information. They can get worn out if they do not take the time to recharge their batteries. They are usually great wits, and can make others laugh by their ability to share the funny and silly sides of life's experiences.

They offer others a deeper perspective on things that they glean from their intuitive natures. Because their minds are so active, they benefit from athletics and exercise to bring them into their bodies. They can be cynical and appear curt.

A sense of humor makes the world go around. Dr. Seuss, Charles Schultz (*Peanuts*), and Walt Kelly (*Pogo* cartoon) were all **6 Metal** personalities. They created children's books and cartoon series that still today entertain the children that read them. Funny rhyming and silly characters coupled with fun pictures and a rich sense of humor is their approach to teaching.

6 METAL PERSONALITIES

	Outer Nature	**Inner Nature**
Bibi Netanyahu	6 Metal	6 Metal
Scott Walker	6 Metal	6 Metal
Tom Brokaw	6 Metal	5 Earth
Morley Safer	6 Metal	5 Earth
Walt Kelly	6 Metal	5 Earth
Dr. Seuss	6 Metal	5 Earth
Charles Schultz	6 Metal	5 Earth
Bob Dole	5 Earth	6 Metal
Peter Jennings	8 Earth	6 Metal
Stephen Miller	6 Metal	8 Earth
James Madison	6 Metal	4 Tree
Walter Cronkite	3 Tree	6 Metal
Michelle Malkin	3 Tree	6 Metal
Margaret Thatcher	3 Tree	6 Metal
Sebastian Gorka	3 Tree	6 Metal
Ayn Rand	6 Metal	3 Tree
Ainsley Earhardt	6 Metal	7 Metal
Ulysses S Grant	7 Metal	6 Metal
Kellyanne Conway	7 Metal	6 Metal
Menachem Begin	7 Metal	6 Metal

Juan Williams	1 Water	6 Metal
Eric Bolling	1 Water	6 Metal
Shepard Smith	1 Water	6 Metal
Mo Brooks	1 Water	6 Metal
Andy Rooney	1 Water	6 Metal
Ed Henry	2 Earth	6 Metal
E Hemingway	2 Earth	6 Metal
Gerald Ford	6 Metal	9 Fire
Roger Ailes	6 Metal	2 Earth
Gio Benitez	6 Metal	6 Metal
Andrea Michell	9 Fire	6 Metal

Tom Brokaw, Ted Koppel, Morley Safer, Dan Rather, Walter Cronkite, Peter Jennings all share the **6 Metal** approach to the news. They are direct and clear. They do not act out the news and rarely express their opinion about the topics. Ed Henry, **2 Earth, 6 Metal**, has the **6 Metal** nature that can seem very official, but he often smiles and uses his **2 Earth** Facial expressions to give away his feelings about the topic at hand.

Roger Ailes influenced how FOX news came across to his listeners. He understood the **2 Earth,** " the Story" approach, and put the "Fair and Balanced" motto front and center. This was official and clear, but he clearly understood how to draw in his audience.

Mo Brooks is a good example of a **6 Metal** personality in today's political arena. He is clear and concise with an inner resolve, but his **1 Water** nature also has an expansive expressive way of looking at the whole dynamics of politics.

Ayn Rand, **6 Metal, 3 Tree**, was a Russian-American novelist, philosopher, playwright, and screenwriter. She is known for her two best-selling novels, *The Fountainhead* and *Atlas Shrugged*, and for developing a philosophical system she called Objectivism.

"Do not let your fire go out, spark by irreplaceable spark in the hopeless swamps of the not-quite, the not-yet, and the not-at-all. Do not let the hero in your soul perish in lonely frustration for the life you deserved and have never been able to reach. The world you desire can be won. It exists... it is real... it is possible... it's yours."

"I could die for you. But I couldn't, and wouldn't, live for you."

"Freedom: To ask nothing. To expect nothing."

"If you don't know, the thing to do is not to get scared, but to learn." depend on nothing."

"Learn to value yourself, which means: fight for your happiness."
    -Ayn Rand, *Fountain Head*

All the **6 Metal** personalities listed are direct and get to the point.

Remember, **Metal** personalities that are also **Tree,** and **Metal-Fire** types, can experience a push pull inside them. One side will tend to override the other. Once this is understood, full potential exists to take advantage of the strengths from both and recognize when this is happening.

BENJAMIN NETANYAHU

The 6 METAL, 6 METAL Personality
The Conduit

Leader, intuitive, forthright, sense of humor, caring, loyal, fixer, fast paced, wants peace, perceptive, protective.

Born to lead, the *6 Metal, 6 Metal* personality may have the propensity to get on the Trump Train if that person feels things can get done for the good of the people. Benjamin Netanyahu's *6 Metal, 6 Metal* nature is to get things done and quickly move to the next problem on the list. He supports President Donald Trump's inner *1 Water* vision of formulating a clear path and standing up for "making America great again." The two men could form a friendship that is sincere and thought provoking.

This was not true about Benjamin Netanyahu, *6 Metal, 6 Metal*, and Obama, *3 Tree, 9 Fire*; these two men could not fit together well in any way, shape, or form, even if they shared the same political views. There would be no easy connection at any level; they would have to work very hard at this relationship. When together, Obama would appear arrogant and Bibi would appear uptight and rigid.

Scott Walker, *6 Metal, 6 Metal*, has the same direct dedication to the people of his state and overcame huge resistance on his way to becoming governor of Wisconsin. He has a clear path and gets it done.

KELLYANNE CONWAY

The 7 METAL, 6 METAL Personality
The Pragmatist/ the Conduit

Sharp, Intense, Verbally succinct, Intuitive. Strong presence, Hard worker, Loyal, Protective Steel belted, Workaholic, Direct, Caring.

Anyone who likes President Trump and voted for him knows he has a warrior in Kellyanne. She is a *7 Metal, 6 Metal* personality type. People of this type are great judges of character and take no prisoners. They stick to the point, are good listeners, and will not waver in exposing what they see as mistruths or half lies. Any TV host on any show or station has a hard time managing her.

Conway has *7 Metal, 6 Metal* wit, a recollection of the truth, and informative insights. Most of all, she does this while smiling and nodding pleasantly. "Go ahead, try me," is the look in her eye. There is no fluff to Conway's *7 Metal, 6 Metal* personality type.

This does not mean she is not very feminine and charming, but it does mean she has an agenda and small talk serves no value to her. I imagine that her home life is similar. She may carry on conversations with her children in the same way she does with adults. Recharging the *7 Metal, 6 Metal* batteries is necessary for this personality type to stay focused and upbeat.

If they follow their intuition, trust their first feelings on things, and do not overthink problems, they will be right on. Conway is a true asset to the Trump administration. She understands Donald Trump's vision and commitment. She appreciates his ability to tell a story, be entertaining, get out in public, and tell it like he sees it.

Her *7 Metal, 6 Metal* personality type is not in his administration because she wants a job or is looking for recognition. She has a personality type that sees where she is needed and fills the void. Kellyanne Conway has no problem wearing the pants, so to speak, and getting the job done. Does she like to be told she did a good job? Of course, everyone likes that, but Donald Trump certainly gives credit where credit is due.

I am sure Donald Trump's **9 Fire** nature keeps things interesting and hard to follow at times. Conway's **7 Metal, 6 Metal** is one of Donald Trump's best assets. She is goal minded, has resolve, and is very intuitive. She would not like the drama in the media or politics; **7 Metal, 6 Metal** personalities find drama distracting and draining. She shares the same personality type, **7 Metal, 6 Metal**, as Ulysses S Grant, the 18th President.

"The art of war is simple enough, find out where your enemy is. Get him as soon as you can. Strike him as hard as you can, and keep moving on."

"Although a soldier by profession, I have never felt any sort of fondness for war, I have never advocated for it, except as a means for peace."

"I know only two tunes: one of them is Yankee Doodle, the other one isn't."

-Ulysses S Grant

Kellyanne, shares Ulysses S Grant's *7 Metal, 6 Metal* personality. She obviously lives in a different time and is not a Soldier in a war, but her objectives are similar and clear. One must fight the battles and there is no sense in sticking toes in to test the water. These types jump in and are ready to defend what they believe in to feel peace in mind.

The 7 METAL Personality

The Pragmatist

7 Metal personalities have a lot going on underneath the surface. They are strong vessels for intuitive or psychic inclinations. *7 Metal* individuals are good at taking things apart and putting things back together. They love to know how things work; what better way than to take something apart and put it back together? They are problem solvers. They will take a lawn mower apart so they can write an instruction manual for others to follow. These tendencies make the *7 Metal* type precise and clear. These types make very good teachers because they know how to take students from A-Z in a practical useful way.

They are attracted to trying things that can be dangerous and exhilarating, just to see if they can do it. They are intuitive and focused; they can pick up on others' weaknesses, when it serves a purpose. Many can be seen playing the Dirty Harry and James Bond type characters in movies. **Clint Eastwood, Gcne Hackman, Cary Grant, Steve McQueen,**

Robert Wagner, and **Sean Connery** all share this edgy personality. Clint Eastwood's "Make my day," *7 metal* nature says it all.

George Washington and **Ulysses S Grant** are great examples of the *7 Metal* personality. Going into battle for a cause, whether in a war or in the courtroom, they are dedicated to getting the job done. They have no problem calling people out if they think they are full of bull. Do not pick a fight with a *7 Metal* because their debating skills are sharp and they are usually informed.

They usually like music, to dance, and to be entertaining. Women *7 Metal* personalities, such as **Ainsley Earhardt** and **Kellyanne Conway**, are very feminine, but also come off as direct and getting right to the point. Both of these women smile as their piercing eyes see right through you.

On *Fox and Friends*, Earhardt's *6 Metal* nature "herds the cats," so to speak, and serves as the fulcrum to support the more demonstrative Brian Kilmeade.

The 3 hosts work very well together. They actually cover all of the personalities on that show. Steve Doocy is an **8 Earth, 3 Tree**, Brian is a **9 Fire, 2 Earth**, and Ainsley is a **6 Metal, 7 Metal** personality.
 The water nature is missing, but Radio and TV forms a water current through which they communicate, so to me they make the perfect mix.

7 METAL PERSONALITIES

	Outer Nature	Inner Nature
Steve McQueen	7 Metal	7 Metal
Gene Hackman	7 Metal	6 Metal
Clint Eastman	7 Metal	5 Earth
Sean Connery	7 Metal	2 Earth
George Washington	7 Metal	8 Earth
John Bolton	7 Metal	8 Earth
Hugh Downs	7 Metal	8 Earth
Katie Hopkins	7 Metal	8 Earth
Harry Reid	7 Metal	8 Earth
Jay Sekulow	8 Earth	7 Metal
Kellyanne Conway	7 Metal	6 Metal
Matt Bevin	7 Metal	6 Metal
Ainsley Earhardt	6 Metal	7 Metal
Bill O'Reilly	6 Metal	7 Metal
Mark Levin	7 Metal	1 Water
John Jay	7 Metal	4 Tree
Larry Arnn	3 Tree	7 Metal
A. Napolitano	5 Earth	7 Metal
Bob Hope	7 Metal	5 Earth
Dolley Madison	7 Metal	5 Earth
Matt Lauer	7 Metal	7 Metal

Wolf Blitzer	7 Metal	7 Metal
Greg Gutfeld	9 Fire	7 Metal
Devin Nunes	9 Fire	7 Metal
Colonel Paterson	9 Fire	7 Metal
Dan Horowitz	1 Water	7 Metal
Julian Assange	2 Earth	7 Metal
George Soros	7 Metal	2 Earth

Mark Levin is a perfect example of an individual who can take apart a topic and put it back together again. His listeners love his ability to examine and offer insights that hit the nail on the head. His *7 Metal* emotional nature never hesitates to call out those who may piss on his foot and say it is raining. He calls a spade a spade.

Larry Arnn is a great example of a *3 Tree* personality that speaks his truth. A great educator, he is the President of Hillsdale College. His *7 Metal* side is masterful at teaching and bringing alive the values of the Constitution and the Founding Fathers' dedication to Liberty for all. His vision bridges the two very different expression of his personality.

Founding Father **John Jay** (1745-1829) served as the first Chief Justice of the U.S. Supreme Court, as well as a variety of other top government posts. The New York native drafted the state's first constitution in 1777 and the following year was chosen as president of the Continental Congress. John Jay was a *7 Metal, 4 Tree* with the same skill set as Larry Arnn. John Jay had the *4 Tree* philosophical inner nature to assist him in his travels. His personality type needed to be totally be in the flow with his vision, or he would be unhappy.

Julian Assange is a controversial figure that exposed the *Wikileaks* emails. His *7 Metal* nature is direct, clear with his intentions, and has an understanding of network systems. His *2 Earth* nature is the part of him that is interested in exposing the "Story." He knows the details that shape the narrative.

MARK LEVIN

The 7 METAL, 1 WATER Personality
The Pragmatist/ The Wave

"Reporting from his Underground bunker" says it all.
**Analytical, Excellent writer, Factual, Teacher,
Calls a spade a spade, Hates fools, Likes intricacy
and systems, Opinionated, Researcher, Fights
for justice, Hates hypocrisy, Can be impatient,
Understands the law, Visionary, Sarcastic,
Pragmatic.**

Mark Levin's *7 Metal* nature never hesitates to say
it like it is. If you are an incompetent boob, he will
be sure to tell you. He is the first to say that he
smells a rat. He devotes a tremendous amount of
research to any subject about which he shares his
thoughts. Levin shares Newt Gingrich's *1 Water*
nature, which means he is able to take his audience
back in time and give the big picture.

Liberty and Justice for all actually means something
to Mark Levin; it may even be written on the outside
of the steel door to his underground bunker.

A friend of mine asked me why he seems to yell his radio show. My thoughts are that, because of his **7 Metal** nature, he feels that his passion for the topic needs to be expressed. Even though many people cannot see his softer side, he does have one.

His **1 Water** nature is natural at writing, inventing, seeing the big picture, imagining the future, and valuing music. Levin cares deeply about those around him who share his cause. He is a big picture **1 Water** thinker. He sees the urgency to rectify and salvage all that has been taken away. He is a **7 Metal** protector of liberty.

His gift as a **7 Metal** is that he is invaluable at dissecting something by taking it apart and putting it back together so the pieces fit perfectly. This is a great teaching tool as well. He makes sense out of the matter at hand. Often, like most **7 Metal** personalities, he lacks tact because he sees no value in it and thinks it is a waste of time. He serves as a Justice Warrior, and his honest straightforward approach is needed in this world where expedience is important. People that love listening to Mark Levin love to learn new things and get a different perspective.

JAY SEKULOW

The 8 EARTH, 7 METAL Personality
The introspect/ The Pragmatist

Freedom fighter, Warrior, Decisive, Debater, Historian, Researcher, Fights for justice, Workaholic, Moral compass. A man on a mission, A rebel with many causes. Believes in religious freedom, Very soulful, Deep, Rich inner life.

The *8 Earth, 7 Metal* type perfectly supports the goals of President Trump, *9 Fire, 1 Water*, and the future of our nation. *8 Earth, 7 Metal* people are grounded, driven, and believe in dissecting the subject at hand.

These types have an *8 Earth* soulful way of looking at things. Their *7 Metal* side is very precise with the words they chose, and does not mind taking up a cause they believe in. Being a lawyer would be easy for Jay Sekulow's personality type, as long as he can stand by his principles.

Our first president, **George Washington**, *7 Metal, 8 Earth,* has the same personality combination as Jay Sekulow, *8 Earth, 7 Metal*, but Washington's outer *KI* nature was *7 Metal*. George Washington presented his more intense *7 Metal* nature on the surface. It makes sense that Donald Trump would be happy to have a George Washington type by his side in this crazy time in history.

Jay Sekulow, *8 Earth, 7 Metal,* does his research, understands the guiding principles, finds the forum to educate, makes it his mission to fight for freedom, and takes out his sword in a heartbeat.

His book on Isis, *The Rise of Isis*, is pertinent for our time. I am sure that there are those who may not like him because, like all *7 Metal* types, he exposes and challenges the facts being presented. Sekulow's words can be cutting and sharp, yet on the surface in his *8 Earth* nature, he appears gentle and thought provoking.

Jay was a fine choice to serve on President Donald
Trump's legal team. President Trump can say to Jay,
"Here you handle this" and feel the matter had been
placed in the right hands. *8 Earth, 7 Metal*
personalities work tirelessly when they take on a
task.

Since he has a Radio show and is a regular
contributor on other TV and media outlets, he offers
valuable insights that are well articulated and
educational. Both sides of his *8 Earth, 7 Metal*
personality benefit from bringing a valuable
message to the public. *8 Earth, 7 Metal* individuals
need to be able to relax in a free-flowing setting at
times to help them decompress. The Radio setting
offers a chance for that flowing expression. *8 Earth,
7 Metal* types do not just state their opinion, they
present facts and support those facts with the law.
The suit he wears is his armor. All Jay needs is a
white horse.

An *8 Earth, 7 Metal,* when in balance, believes in
faith and justice for all. Since *8 Earth, 7 Metals* are

tenacious and pragmatic, Sekulow's nature is a driving force in his pursuit for justice. There is so much more to say about each of the personality types. We are looking at only a small glimpse into these personality types and the insights that I offer to my clients.

Sekulow's personality type needs something in his life that allows him to decompress and calm his mind. It is likely that Sekulow benefits from being around the water, sailing, or going out in nature for a little nurturing of the soul and exercise.

"If anyone tells you that you cannot legislate morality, remember that legislation IS morality."

-Jay Sekulow

Harry Reid, *7 Metal, 8 Earth*, was a driving force for his cause and a life-long career politician. The *7 Metal, 8 Earth* is a very strong personality type, and he had a lot of influence over those in the Democrat party during his very long stay in his position. His agenda was a driving force from 1999-2015. He knew what he wanted and went after it.

Reid took many liberties in his influential position to lobby for support for agendas he felt were important. His critics say his *7 Metal* hardline agenda was more about padding his pockets than the interests of the people. He made a lot of money using taxpayer funds in spending bills to do things like building a bridge between Nevada and Arizona. His critics say that it was earmarked spending to make his land more valuable. For good or for bad, no one can say he was not a strong force in the

Democrat party. His fortitude and drive is a good example of the *7 Metal, 8 Earth* personality that never gives up the goal at hand. You will read about the *8 Earth* personality on the next page.

The 8 EARTH Personality

The Introspect

The Trigram in the *I Ching* for this type is the **Mountain**. Often, **8 Earth** types are deep inside themselves, contemplating and appearing like they are far away.

They seek peace of mind, but in this world, peace is hard to find, so inner peace is necessary for an **8 Earth** to feel peaceful. **8 Earth** people are drawn to professions and lifestyles that can isolate them, like being a Monk. Of course, this is not true if they are **9 Fire** as well. Fire people need to shine in the limelight.

8 Earth personalities are very grounded, can be stubborn, and stand their ground. They are detailed, want all the facts, and continually seek to gather information. **8 Earth** people care deeply about those who are closest to them, but they can get overwhelmed if others ask too much of them when they are not ready. They can offer much to a relationship and to the people they work with if they believe in what they are doing. Condi Rice is a perfect example of the strength of an **8 Earth** offering assistance in the background. She is smart, knowledgeable, and grounded, which you see in her **8 Earth** nature. Her **1 Water** nature is free flowing, and looks at the bigger picture. Once she gains clarity, she moves forward.

The **8 Earth** personality is contemplative and does not mind being alone. **8 Earth** types ponder existence and appreciate the fact that we are just a small speck in the universe. Being outdoors is a good chance for **8 Earth** types to recharge their batteries. Learning about natural occurrences that are happening all the time interests them. They are drawn to educating themselves about what exists beyond their immediate situation, whether it be around the world or in the wild. They appreciate things like observing bears in their natural habitat, watching salmon head upstream, or learning how things have evolved over the years.

8 Earth people are very introspective and, if the other part of their personality is **9 Fire**, **3 Tree** or

4 Tree, they constantly struggle with wanting to go inward and be contemplative. *9 Fire, 3 Tree* and *4 Tree* types want to be out in the world, moving and shaking. For example, if a person is *8 Earth, 3 Tree*, the *3 Tree* nature seeks the new and curiosity pulls them up and out. The *8 Earth* wants to retreat inward, so there is a push pull within the personality.

If *6* or *7 Metal* is the other personality, an *8 Earth* person will always be on the move, so the *8 Earth* side will feel a bit resistant to the action-packed nature of the Metal side. Combining a *6* or *7 Metal* nature with the *8 Earth* nature means the train will move forward and the metal nature wants to get things done. When the metal side feels that enough information has been gathered, decisions can be made and implemented. Balancing both sides of their nature is key to the happiness of these types.

The *8 Earth, 1 Water* personality struggles with wanting to expand and see the broader view, while also striving to be practical and detailed. If an individual is aware of the strengths of each, both sides can be valuable.

8 EARTH PERSONALITIES

	Outer Nature	Inner Nature
Ben Franklin	8 Earth	3 Tree
Pat Buchanan	8 Earth	3 Tree
Chris Wallace	8 Earth	3 Tree
Steve Doocy	8 Earth	3 Tree
Tom Cotton	5 Earth	8 Earth
Scott Pruitt	5 Earth	8 Earth
John Kelly	5 Earth	8 Earth
Henry Kissinger	5 Earth	8 Earth
Mike Lee	2 Earth	8 Earth
Larry Kudlow	8 Earth	5 Earth
Dan Bongino	8 Earth	2 Earth
Ronald Reagan	8 Earth	2 Earth
Trey Gowdy	9 Fire	8 Earth
Sarah Sanders	9 Fire	8 Earth
Mike Huckabee	9 Fire	8 Earth
Jay Sekulow	8 Earth	7 Metal
John Bolton	7 Metal	8 Earth
Peter Jennings	8 Earth	6 Metal

Stephen Miller	6 Metal	8 Earth
Callista Gingrich	7 Metal	8 Earth
John Kennedy	2 Earth	8 Earth
Marilyn Monroe	2 Earth	8 Earth
Mitch McConnell	4 Tree	8 Earth
Maxine Waters	8 Earth	5 Earth
Joe Manchin	8 Earth	5 Earth
Bill Clinton	9 Fire	8 Earth
Kim Jong Un	8 Earth	9 Fire
Mitt Romney	8 Earth	1 Water

8 Earth, 5 Earth and *5 Earth, 8 Earth* individuals are often drawn to leadership roles and running for office is something they might enjoy. *5 Earth* people like being in the center of things and teamwork gives them energy. People like **Maxine Waters** and **Joe Manchin** love to be in charge and are attracted to being in politics.

Mitch McConnell and **Joe Biden** share the same *4 Tree, 8 Earth* personality type. Both McConnell and Biden are perfect examples of appearing fully engaged on a topic one moment and null and void the next.

Their outer *4 Tree* natures appear to support active
and groundbreaking opportunities, while the other
8 Earth side retreats to a more cautious status quo
position. A leadership position is not easy for either
of these men. This does not mean that they do not
have their own skill sets. This dynamic is currently
playing out in the Senate; one wonders if there is no
conviction to get on the train, because it seems they
feel just fine sitting at the station.

A stronger personality would be helpful. Politics
often requires someone who can stand front and
center with a compelling message that the people of
the United States need things fixed. However,
urgency does not exist in **Mitch McConnell**'s
toolbox to fix the problem.

This does not mean that an *8 Earth* personality is
not able to fight for a cause. It does mean both sides
of their personalities need to be a united front, with
no push pull going on inside them. Take **Dan
Bongino**, a conservative who has served his
country. He is a rebel with a cause, which is
expressed in his *8 Earth* nature.

His **2 Earth** inner nature is emotional and he cannot speak quickly enough to get out all his feelings and frustrations about the government. He has a strong sense of purpose, and he is able to share his thoughts on the radio and on paper. These actions support his personality type. He may need to slow his pace down and seem less frantic so that his listeners can take in all that he is sharing about.

Ronald Reagan had the same **8 Earth, 2 Earth** personality type, but because he was an actor, he had learned to slow down when speaking and use his **8 Earth** nature to deliver his message. Watching himself on the big screen gave him the feedback he needed to become calm and controlled. He used his **2 Earth** nature to tell a story and share his feelings, but his **8 Earth** nature was able to project and convey his thoughts to the public. Reagan is a perfect example of the inner and outer natures working together.

It is common for **8 Earth** persons to be on the Right, more conservative side of politics. **Larry Kudlow,**

8 Earth, 5 Earth, **Tom Cotton**, *5 Earth, 8 Earth,*
and **Scott Pruitt**, *5 Earth, 8 Earth*, are all drawn to
being fiscally conservative. Budgeting is a part of
their skill sets. They see the need to let people
budget themselves and favor smaller government.
This echoes Ronald Reagan's *8 Earth* sentiment
exactly.

 The problem in politics is that when a person
becomes charge of the "people's money" in
authoritative positions like the Senate and
Congress. Personalities like Maxine Waters and Joe
Manchin, both *8 Earth, 5 Earth*, on the Left use
authoritative powers to dictate where the "people's
money" should go, to whom, and how much should
be collected through taxation. This is playing out in
the forefront of politics today more than ever.

Trey Gowdy, another *8 Earth* personality, has a
personality that combines both *9 Fire* and *8 Earth*.
He has an *8 Earth* fact-gathering nature. He is very
clear, purposeful, and has done his homework. His
9 Fire nature makes him very comfortable on stage
or in the public eye. Since *8 Earth* is his outer
nature,

that is what people see. His fiery side is more hidden and only shows in personal settings.

Kim Jong-un, *8 Earth, 9 Fire*, loves his position in North Korea. He loves being in the limelight and also being in charge of his own safety and inner circle. So much more could be said about this dictator's personality.

JOHN KELLY

THE 5 EARTH, 8 EARTH Personality
The Center/ The Introspect

Authoritative, Collector of information, Introspective, Soulful, In control, Reflective. A lot of thought goes into his decision-making, Grounded.

John Kelly is a person who acts on experience, and watches for pitfalls in the road ahead. Having served in the military, he would never take lightly the threats that exist today. He is a very grounded *5 Earth, 8 Earth*; both his outer nature and his inner nature are hard to move away from things he feels strongly about.

Kelly's introspective *8 Earth* nature makes him a deep person and when he speaks, it is with authority. When he brings his *5 Earth* gathering of information to the table, it comes with a lot of thought and information to back it up. He takes his job very seriously and is perhaps thought of as stubborn and opinionated at times.

5 Earth personalities are drawn to the military and to being in politics. Kelly is hard to move off a goal if he believes in what he is doing. He does not care what obstacles get in his way. Most *8 Earth* personalities love to be in nature, and have no problem being alone. This type may enjoy a cabin on a mountaintop or a fishing trip in Alaska. They like to chill out with responsibilities for none but themselves. However, Kelly's *8 Earth* does not want to let anyone down and he cares deeply, so he would never rest for too long. He also uses his *5 Earth* nature to look at all sides of a problem.

He is a warrior for safety and a great personality choice for his job. Trump can pass along orders and they will be followed. The *5 Earth, 8 Earth* personality needs others on a team to take care of the paperwork, finalize work, implement marching orders, and get things done. Kelly is better at organizing the posse and then giving everyone a role to achieve the goal at hand. Kelly excels at handing out a plan to others working in their roles for the common good.

Henry Kissinger is also a *5 Earth, 8 Earth* personality.

HILLARY CLINTON

The 8 EARTH, 3 TREE Personality
The Introspect / The Thunderous

Hillary Clinton craves the limelight and wishes she had the **9 Fire** charisma that Bill has. Her **8 Earth** nature is best operating behind the scenes, not having to be out acting pleasant and friendly.

She is not a chit chatty person, and does not care about getting to know other people, per say. I don't necessarily mean this in a mean way; Clinton knows it already. Of course, she enjoys talking with those she wants to talk to, but having to mingle with the masses is not something she would enjoy. She would be more at ease on a panel of experts or being interviewed to give her opinion.

Her **8 Earth** side is introspective and her **3 Tree** inner nature wants to be able to say it like it is, with no filter. This does not mean that she does not care about those around her; it means she is not a warm and fuzzy personality. That is why she appears to be yelling when she is speaking to the public.

8 Earth, 3 Tree people do not get charged up about having to mince words or worry about delivery.

Being president would totally fit her idea of what makes her happy. Hillary Clinton craves what bridges the two sides of her nature, which is getting the accolades and attention of being president. If she did not have to go on the darn campaign trail and be friendly and eat meals with the folks, all would be great. Both sides of her nature hate the thought of the campaign trail.

She already has her own idea of what is good for the people and she would have been tickled pink to just get to work and have a spokesperson go out to talk to the people. She craves power and loves the idea of running the show.

Loving the ideology of Saul Alinsky, Hillary Clinton finds some appeal in a control-the-masses, communism-style approach to politics. Bill Clinton, Obama, and Saul Alinsky share the **9 Fire** magnetic charisma. All three men have effective public speaking appeal, but Hillary does not.

If Hillary Clinton were being truly honest and true to herself, she would have said something like this on the campaign:

*Hello Americans, I know what is best for you.
Please just let me do my job and I will take care of everything. My Husband was a good president and he will help with the things that he is good at.*

*Forgive me. I really do not have time for chitchat. I am not warm and fuzzy but Chelsea, my daughter, is very chatty and she will be glad to come out to talk with you. She loves to share stories as a **2 Earth, 2 Earth**, and talk to everyone. She will come back and tell me how you feel. She is a great listener too.*

I will do a great job and please understand I have been at this all my life; you are in good hands. I did not always like the positions I had, but it got me where I am today. Rest assured you are taken care of. Being President has always been my dream.

*Thank You.
Hillary*

The 9 FIRE Personality
The Flamboyant

The **9 Fire** personality is expressive and can be very charismatic. This is the "Here I am, world" personality. When you think of fire you think of flames flickering, spreading light. **9 Fire** types are social butterflies and have a natural stage presence. They expand as far as they can until they hit the boundary line. If there are no boundaries set, these people will keep expanding.

9 Fire children love showing off and being on stage. If they have very controlling or demanding parents, **9 Fires** can become shy and afraid to be their naturally flamboyant selves. So, there is a fine line to walk for the parents of a **9 Fire** child. They crave boundaries, yet they need the room to be their naturally gregarious selves.

They want to be recognized and work hard at making a name for themselves. They even enjoy getting notoriety, as bad attention can be just as rewarding as good attention for some **9 Fires.**

Most *9 Fire* personalities make great salesmen or women. The old saying, "They could sell a bag of ice to an Eskimo" applies to the *9 Fire* personality.

Nineteen out of forty-five of the presidents of the United States have had *9 Fire* personalities. Of course, the *9 Fire* nature manifests differently in each person, due to the combination of his or her inner and outer natures. These types are drawn to the presidential position.

Someone like Susan Rice, *9 Fire, 5 Earth*, and Eric Holder, *5 Earth, 9 Fire*, loved the positions they held in the Obama administration. The *5 Earth* part of their natures is drawn to holding a high position in the government, and being in charge where their opinions are important.

Since Obama, *3 Tree, 9 Fire*, shares their *9 Fire* nature, they worked well with him. Obama's strong, front-and-center campaign manager David Axelrod was another *9 Fire, 5 Earth* combination. He has an in-your-face attitude when it comes to running a campaign.

Bill Hemmer on *Fox* and David Muir on *ABC*, both
9 Fire, 5 Earth, enjoy the positions they are in on
TV, being up front and center.

9 FIRE PERSONALITIES

	Outer Nature	Inner Nature
Thomas Jefferson	5 Earth	9 Fire
Rush Limbaugh	5 Earth	9 Fire
Bill Hemmer	9 Fire	5 Earth
Winston Churchill	9 Fire	5 Earth
Brian Williams	9 Fire	5 Earth
Glenn Beck	9 Fire	5 Earth
Wilbur Ross	9 Fire	5 Earth
Jim Jordan	9 Fire	5 Earth
Jay Leno	5 Earth	9 Fire
Brian Kilmeade	9 Fire	2 Earth
Rand Paul	2 Earth	9 Fire
Jared Kushner	2 Earth	9 Fire
Norah O'Donnell	9 Fire	3 Tree
Gregg Jarrett	9 Fire	3 Tree
Greg Gutfeld	9 Fire	7 Metal
Ed Sullivan	9 Fire	7 Metal

Dave Brat	9 Fire	9 Fire
Lindsey Graham	9 Fire	9 Fire
Trey Gowdy	9 Fire	8 Earth
Robert Redford	9 Fire	8 Earth
Bill Gates	9 Fire	6 Metal
Huma Abedin	6 Metal	9 Fire
Bret Baier	3 Tree	9 Fire
John Adams	4 Tree	9 Fire
Donald Trump	9 Fire	1 Water
Sarah H. Sanders	9 Fire	8 Earth
Mike Huckabee	9 Fire	8 Earth

Along with 19 of the presidents of the United States.

Greg Gutfeld, **9 Fire, 7 Metal**, is the perfect example of a personality type that loves the limelight. You can see he enjoys being animated and entertaining, which shows his **9 Fire** personality. He also is a **7 Metal**, which is evident in his snarky and sarcastic analysis; he calls a spade a spade. On *Fox*, he offers a well-researched approach to what he says, with a charismatic sense of humor.

Why Obama and Bill Clinton had easy times getting elected. This even applies to George W. Bush, who, though he had a harder time than these others, still made it to the Presidency.

The last 4 presidents have had *9 Fire* as either their outer nature or their inner emotional nature. 19 out of 45 presidents have had the fire nature in their personality type.

The *9 Fire* personality loves being in the limelight, exudes charisma, is entertaining, and enjoys an audience. These types love attention, and have no problem being heartfelt, dramatic, and are very comfortable performing on stage.

Many of our entertainers and comics today are *9 Fire* personalities. Acting comes easily to a *9 Fire* personality.

9 Fire personalities have a charismatic passion for a topic and are entertaining, whether you like them or not. With that said, let's look at each of the last elected presidents .

BILL CLINTON

The 9 FIRE, 8 EARTH Personality
The Flamboyant/ The Mountain

Bill Clinton's outer *9 Fire* nature is full of charisma and charm, and has a heartfelt story to go with it. He is entertaining and loves to put on a good show. His *9 Fire* nature loves attention and being in the limelight. On the inside, he is much more introspective. His inner nature is *8 Earth,* which is deep thinking, introspective, grounded, and enjoys gathering all of the information needed to make a decision. He has the ability to appear grounded, convincing and controlled, as well as to be very entertaining. He as a *9 Fire* who can light up the room and an *8 Earth* who can control the narrative.

Bill Clinton goes through life with a continual struggle on his hands. He is a scoundrel and Samaritan all in one person. This is not an easy combination to be, but it works well for being elected the president of the United States. The *9*

Fire personality is charismatic, and can be captivating while telling a story. Who better to tell stories about growing, meeting Hillary, and sharing an *8 Earth*, just-a-regular-Joe storyline?

Those on the Left saw his sweet charm and heartfelt concern. Those on the Right often said he is full of Baloney and wondered how anyone could fall for that crap.

Even so, many ladies on the Right say he is so charming and that it feels like he is speaking directly to you. He would be able to morph into being like the person he is speaking to; he has no problem saying what the person or crowd wants to hear.

GEORGE W. BUSH

THE 1 WATER, 9 FIRE Personality
The Water/ the Flamboyant

You might say, "No way, he is not a **9 Fire,** he does not act like Bill Clinton." Keep in mind, however, the two men often go on talk shows together and say they are brothers from different mothers.

George Bush is very entertaining when he is relaxed and able to show his *9 Fire* inner nature. He is a *1 Water, 9 Fire*. Thus, he is not natural at being in the limelight and struggled while reading the teleprompter. He would have been much better off just articulating his thoughts, relaxed in a fireside chat setting.

His *1 Water* outer nature was in the forefront throughout his presidency; this was what he presented to the world. His *9 Fire* personality was most prominent when 9.11 happened. At this time, he had passion and resolve; he spoke from his heart and had his 6-shooter at the ready to take down terrorists. He was FIRED up.

Water puts out fire. Because one side of George Bush is reserved, easy going, and likes looking at the bigger picture, his inner **9 Fire** nature easily gets doused or pushed to the back burner, by his water nature. He is likely happier being on his ranch or doing speaking engagements with Bill Clinton.

Nevertheless, running for president was something he succeeded at. He saw what was needed at the time: a clear vision and purpose. Having a direct conversation with George Bush, one on one, would be far different than watching him on the TV. People that know him say he is very personable.

BARACK OBAMA

The 3 TREE, 9 FIRE Personality
The Thunderous/ The flamboyant

Barack is a *3 Tree, 9 Fire* personality. This makes him a *3 Tree* fighter and also someone who can engage the people by expressing the passion and charisma in his *9 Fire* nature. He has a true stage presence. He can pound his agenda with direct articulate points and then throw on the charm and fanfare.

Even Chris Matthews gets tingles listening to him. Obama has all the ingredients to be a dynamo on stage, and his *3 Tree* nature gets crowds worked up. He has charisma and a good speechwriter, Ben Rhodes, who has a *2 Earth* personality and the skill set to create the "Story." Rhodes is responsible for the tears and tragedy aspect of Obama's speeches. This comes right out of the Alinsky/Obama, *Rules for Radicals*, rulebook.

"Rub raw the sores of discontent, cause more division and add the emotional story to be told."

-Saul Alinsky

The Obamas are not warm and fuzzy emotional personality types, but thanks to their speech writers, all of their speeches are. That does not mean the Obamas are not loving demonstrative parents. It does mean that they have a secret weapon in speechwriter Rhodes, a *2 Earth*. Rhodes was on staff to tweet regularly and keep the Obamas in the forefront of people's minds by expressing that they still care about the people.

Obama had control over drama and also a mission. Once he was elected into office, Obama pushed his agenda with relentless drive: one goal and one direction. He used every card in the deck. Those on the left wanted to kiss his feet. Those on the right were amazed that he could say and do the things he did. They saw him as deleterious to liberty and freedom. They believed his agenda intentionally caused more division, and was not a good approach for uniting the country.

Sarah Huckabee Sanders and her father *Mike Huckabee* are both *9 Fire, 8 Earth* personalities. Mike Huckabee's *8 Earth* nature is visible in his strong faith and his strong devotion to his ministry. His *9 Fire* entertaining charismatic sense of humor keeps his listeners interested in the topics he discusses. He is knowledgeable and not afraid of the limelight. Being fiscally conservative comes easily to him because most *8 Earths* are very detailed and want to know where the money is being spent and for what. His quotes below show his wit and his love of the country.

Sarah has the same off-the-cuff sense of humor and dedication to our president. She also has a great press room presence. She combines a soulful *8 Earth* concern for the country and with a *9 Fire* charismatic delivery in her pressroom briefings.

"The health care system is really designed to reward you for being unhealthy. If you are a healthy person and work hard to be healthy, there are no benefits."

"You know, in my hometown of Hope, Arkansas, the three sacred heroes were Jesus, Elvis, and FDR, not necessarily in that order."

"I wish we would all remember that being American is not just about the freedom we have; it is about those who gave it to us."

-Mike Huckabee

Together all the 9 Ki personalities each bring their own unique set of talents to support each other to achieve the common goal. When each team member is recognized for the strengths he or she brings to the project, the project will be successful.

1 Water individuals are inventive, have vision and are insightful. They can look at all the angles of the situation. They offer the initial idea, and continual input to keep things evolving.

2 Earth individuals use their skills to bring team members together to hash out the details. Their emphasis is on obtaining a harmonious outcome for all working on any particular project. The tendency of any 2 Earth individuals is to consider all that is involved.

3 Tree individuals want to get all the facts out in the open efficiently and quickly get to the point. They care less about consensus. Their high energy level keeps any project alive and moving. Their enthusiasm and vitality is contagious.

4 Tree individuals add the philosophical approach. They are continually on a quest to broaden their skills. They bring worldliness to the project and their input is well rounded.

5 *Earth* individuals are solid and love being in charge, they gravitate to being at the center of the the project. They are good at gathering needed information and delegating tasks to other team members.

6 *Metal* individuals add the endurance and focus needed to get things done. They are able to take the information that has been gathered and they take the ball and run with in to bring things to completion.

7 *Metal* individuals are highly focused. They work on the mechanics of the project, how things can be made simple and be taken apart and put back together. They have a great gift for making complex things seem simple.

8 *Earth* individuals provide a solid ground for others to stand on, and often keep to themselves. When others are panicking they offer sensibility and calm advice.

9 *Fire* individuals enjoy being at the center of the public relations aspect of the organization. Making connections within the community and spreading the enthusiasm needed in public relations.

Conclusion

The information contained in this book represents a cursory look into the complexity of each of the personality types.

No single personality type that is better or worse than another. It all depends on what you want to do in life and how you use your *KI* nature to best support your goals. I highlighted well-known political and media figures because they are front and center in our lives.

If you wish to learn more about this subject and gain greater insight into your own personality types, I encourage you to do so. You will be able to embrace your strengths to the greatest advantage. Equally, you will be able to learn the things that drain your life force and seek support and benefit from outside sources.

I do not like to see people waste time beating themselves up, trying to be someone that they are not.

I love when I get calls from parents that tell me they want to understand their children better. They are perplexed by the fact that their children are so very different from their siblings, as well as themselves. How could that be true when they came from the same parents and were brought up in the same home in the same way? We all know that knowledge is power, and deeper knowledge of their own **KI** and those of the people around them can help tremendously.

This book barely scratches the surface of the **KI** personality types. Back in the 90's I was often called to offer insights into the personality dynamics operating in big corporations to develop a plan to support the common goal. Understanding the strengths and weaknesses of each of an office's personnel is invaluable to better achieving goals.

If you are interested in finding more about your personality type, I would be happy to speak with you.

My future books and website Kipersonalities.com will offer additional information to those who wish to learn this system.

Understanding yourself, your family, friends, and co-workers will quickly make a huge difference in what you can expect of them.

I have been living and writing about this system for over 25 years, since I first had the opportunity to formally study the *I Ching* and the **KI** personality types. Feel free to contact me on my website for consultations and classes. sally@sallyfretwell.com

www.ingramcontent.com/pod-product-compliance
Lightning Source LLC
Chambersburg PA
CBHW072006040426
42447CB00009B/1517